FUEL UP

WITH LAIRD HAMILTON

GLOBAL RECIPES FOR
HiGH-PERFORMANCE HUMANS

Authors: Laird Hamilton and William Cawley
Preface: Gabrielle Reece
Recipe Generation: Laird Hamilton, William Cawley and Gabrielle Reece
Recipe Testing, Food Preparation, Cooking & Food Styling: Sharla Barrett
Art Direction and Props Styling: William Cawley
Food Photography: Jennifer Cawley
Lifestyle Photography: Jennifer Cawley
Producers: Two Feet South

Special thanks to: Gabrielle Reece, Selena Souders, Nils Barrett,
Julian Borra, Kenna Colburn, Brian Good, Kolo Kai Organic Farm,
Laird Apparel, Laird Superfood & XPT.

© 2018 Assouline Publishing
3 Park Avenue, 27th floor
New York, NY 10016   USA
Tel.: 212-989-6769   Fax: 212-647-0005
www.assouline.com

Art Director: Jihyun Kim
Designer: Charlotte Sivrière
Editorial Director: Esther Kremer
Editor: Taylor Viens
Photo Editor: Hannah Hayden

ISBN: 9781614286943
Printed in China.

two feet south

FUEL UP

WITH LAIRD HAMILTON

GLOBAL RECIPES FOR
HiGH-PERFORMANCE HUMANS

ASSOULINE

CONTENTS

Opposite page: I enjoy the whole process of gathering and preparing food, and of course taking "the fuel" on board.
Following pages: My backyard for six months of the year: The Bowl, Hanalei Bay, Kauai.

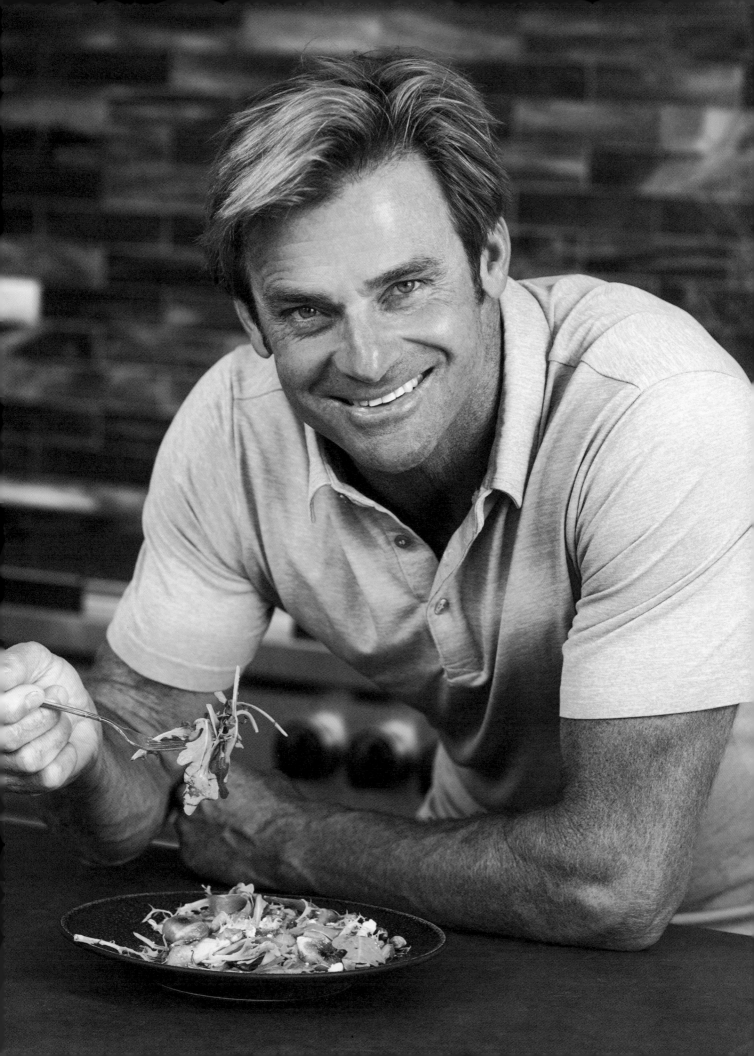

PREFACE

With the abundance of articles and stories published about Laird Hamilton, the intention of this book was to focus on what goes into the body of such an extraordinary athlete and human being. The resulting book is a very personal, and purposely eclectic, collection of recipes that underscores his broad interests in the variety, provenance, and effectiveness of food. Laird's list of priorities is pretty straightforward: waves, family, community, health, and food. Depending on what time of day it is, food might even move right to the top of that list. I have had the pleasure of cooking with him for 22 years, and I've been inspired by his motivation to use the best "fuel" available to power him through a multitude of memorable adventures.

Laird does not approach food in a militant way. He is simply trying to get his hands on the most nutrient-dense and delicious food he possibly can. Our family eating habits are essentially Paleolithic, but we try to avoid being too strict, because it makes you vulnerable. When it comes to food, Laird has several sayings: "If it wasn't here 10,000 years ago, don't eat it." "Avoid the three white devils: white sugar, white flour, and white milk." And, "If you can't pronounce it, don't eat it." When people inquire as to what we eat, my most common response is "plants and animals."

> **"HE RELISHES EATING LOCALLY WHENEVER POSSIBLE, NOT ONLY FOR HIGH-POWERED FUEL, BUT AS A WAY TO LEARN MORE ABOUT, AND COEXIST HARMONIOUSLY WITH THAT ENVIRONMENT."**

Laird's diverse tastes are rooted in his experiences as a world traveler. His profession has taken him to all corners of the world, and every year the list grows longer. When traveling to a new region, one of Laird's favorite things is for locals to share their traditional foods. Laird uses mealtime as a way to connect with friends, family, and his environment. He cherishes the meal not only as a nurturing gesture, but as one of the most fundamental exchanges we use to show our humanity. This book looks to navigate some of these far-off destinations and the waves that live at the heart of them.

These waves have not yet all been ridden by Laird, but as his journey continues he will always find the right equipment to try the local spots, whether they be large, small, cold, warm, bleak or tropical.

Everyone says they won't speak for their partner, but just this once I will. I know that Laird's intention for this cook book, his first book in 10 years, is to share some of his favorite recipes and to give you ideas about using food to serve yourself and your family. This book is not about telling you how to eat or what is best for you; it's simply about provoking curiosity and encouraging you to continue to explore, learn, and stay creative with your food.

These recipes reflect a conventional three-meals-per-day format, but we refer to them as "Sessions," because for Laird personally, "fuel" is not necessarily taken in following the standard timetable. In fact, during the big-wave season in Hawaii, from October to April, he generally does not eat breakfast. His first foray into the water is powered solely by significant quantities of coffee enhanced with Superfood creamers. The rhythm of life is always changing depending on what is transpiring, the season, and one's stage of life. There may be days when you start with a full breakfast, and other times when coffee does the trick until lunch.

"THE KEY IS TO BE IN TOUCH WITH, AND TRUST, WHAT FEELS THE BEST FOR YOU AS AN INDIVIDUAL. IT IS HELPFUL TO DO SOME EXPLORATION AND TRY ALL TYPES OF FOODS AND WAYS OF EATING TO INTIMATELY KNOW YOUR OWN TRUTH. "

In our home, we experiment all the time, and as we continue to learn and progress, we change the foods we eat or choose to eliminate. To understand Laird is to see beyond the athlete and to know the curious innovator. For those of you familiar with Laird's passion for health and food, you will find surprises in this book—from comfort foods like classic roast chicken, and sometimes with creative twists like the fried bananas—but the recipes

are consistently inspiring and nutritionally conscious. We hope that the added dimension of more than fifty special wave spots provokes an interest to keep you exploring our wondrous planet.

One thing Laird always talks about is how, regardless of our age, it is essential to "retain our youthful enthusiasm and curiosity." He approaches his nutrition and eating the same way: always questioning and experimenting with all types of foods, roots, lichen, mushrooms. The list goes on and on. I have seen him eat some pretty intense stuff when someone has told him that it could be good for you. This book is not about following fads or trends. The idea of eating organic, local, real food whenever we can seems like a pretty solid start. Becoming nervous or stressed out around food is not the objective. After all, this is a guy whose New Year's resolution every year is "to laugh more and have more fun."

Is he disciplined? Beyond. Is he motivated by his passion to chase waves for as long as he walks the planet? Absolutely. I don't believe these things have to be in conflict with enjoying yourself and your life. I have said many times that those of us who have the good fortune to be around Laird on a day-to-day basis draft off his incredible passion and energy for life. He is a person who has routinely inspired me to be my best. He has never been about being perfect; he has always been about being authentic and giving it all he's got. So from our family to yours, I wish you vitality, adventure, and many beautiful meals together.

Opposite page: With my better half, Gabrielle, at home on Paradise Cove beach, Malibu.
Pages 16-17: When the waves are not performing I'll grab my race board and go for some mileage before breakfast.

P33 - ALEUTIAN - Alaska

P41 - CHESTERMAN - Canada

P118 - GRAND HAVEN - USA

P34 - HALF MOON - USA
P106 - LITTLE DUME - USA
P65 - FIRST POINT - USA

P55 - HANALEI BAY - Kauai
P126 - HAIKU - MAUI   P84 - WAIMEI - Oahu
P125 - KAHALUU - KONA   P110 - BANYANS - KONA

P130 - SHIPWRECKS - MEXICO   P94 - YUMURI - Cuba

P20 - ESCONDIDO - Mexico

P114 - CHICAMA - Peru

P52- MULLAGHMORE - Ireland

P16 - LUSTY GLAZE - England
P117 - LA CHAPELLE - France
P88 - LA TORCHE - France
P38 - LES CAVALIERS - France
P48 - MUNDAKA - Spain

P99 - SUPERTUBAS - Portugal

P66 - IMSOUANE - Morocco
P30 - ANCHOR POINT - Morocco

P129 - HIGGINS - USA
P23 - DITCH PLAINS - USA

P74 - IPANEMA - Brazil

P56 - PLAYA GRANDE - Argentina

MARETTI - Italy
P71 - KALO NERO - Greece
P29 - NIJIMA - Japan
P62 - UCHIUMI - Japan
P26 - SHIMEI BAY - China
P109 - KAMALA - Thailand
P97 - HONKY'S - Maldives
P113 - GREEN BOWL - Bal.
P91 - KERAMAS - Bali
P61 - CLOUDBREAK - Fiji
P81 - PAPARA - Tahiti
P100 - TEMAE - Tahiti
P87 - POINT VENUS - Tahiti
P78 - SUPERBANK - Australia
P19 - WILD COAST - South Africa
P103 - TRIGG POINT - Australia
P121 - BONDI - AUSTRALIA
P77 - RAGLAN - New Zealand

FIRST SESSION

LUSTY GLAZE BLENDED PORRIDGE WITH BLUEBERRIES & PUMPKIN SEEDS

LUSTY GLAZE, CORNWALL, ENGLAND

An exposed beach break with consistent surf year-round, this Newquay cove is considered by many to be the most beautiful beach in Britain.

Typically British, this homemade porridge is a great start to the day: a nutrient-dense, custom-grain cereal, including protein-packed nuts and topped off with fresh blueberries, which are rich in anthocyanin, a flavanoid with potent antioxidants.

SERVES 2 - TOTAL TIME: 15 MIN

Ingredients for the porridge blend:

4 cups oats

½ cup quinoa

½ cup flaxseeds

1 ½ cups walnuts

1 ½ cups almonds

2 tsp vanilla extract

¼ cup Laird Superfood creamer (optional)

Ingredients for the toppings:

2 cups preferred milk (almond, coconut, soy)

1 cup blueberries, or preferred fruit

½ cup pumpkin seeds, or preferred seeds

TO MAKE THE PORRIDGE BLEND, place the ingredients in a food processor and blend to your desired consistency. I prefer it to be reasonably fine, like a uniform breadcrumb mix. You can make larger quantities and store for weeks in an airtight container. The addition of my Laird Superfood Creamer makes for a really creamy texture, with the benefits of mineral-rich Aquamin.

TO MAKE THE PORRIDGE, warm up 2 cups milk in a small pan over low heat. When hot, add 2 cups porridge blend and simmer, stirring constantly for 5 minutes.

TO SERVE, divide the porridge between two bowls and top each with ½ cup of blueberries and ¼ cup pumpkin seeds.

WILD COAST SAUSAGE WITH SCRAMBLED EGGS, CHERRY TOMATOES, SPINACH & WILD RICE

WILD COAST, EASTERN CAPE, SOUTH AFRICA

I have not surfed here, but this coast is famous for being home to some of the most remote surfing locations in the country. There are still some hidden breaks to discover, albeit a mission to navigate—added to which you are deep into great white shark territory. I love a breakfast scramble—often made with four eggs for me alone! In South Africa they have the *boerewoers* or "farmer sausage," made from a mixture of very lean meats. But pick your own favorite sausage, and slice it into this morning feast.

SERVES 2 - TOTAL TIME: 45 MIN

6 eggs

1 green onion

½ tsp garlic powder

Pinch of ground cumin

Pinch of paprika

Sea salt and black pepper

½ tsp raw butter
  or vegetable oil

2 precooked sausages
  of your choice, sliced

2 packed cups spinach

1 cup cherry tomatoes

1 cup cooked wild rice

WHISK THE EGGS in a medium bowl; stir in the green onion, garlic powder, cumin, paprika, salt, and pepper.

HEAT A LARGE NONSTICK PAN over medium heat; grease it lightly with raw butter or vegetable oil. Add the egg mixture and cook, stirring constantly, for about 5 minutes, until eggs are cooked through.

ADD THE SAUSAGE, spinach, and cherry tomatoes. Reduce the heat to low and cover pan until sausage is heated and the spinach has wilted.

ADD THE WILD RICE and gently stir into the scramble. Serve immediately.

ESCONDIDO BREAKFAST BURRITO WITH CHORIZO, EGGS, BEANS, AVOCADO & PICO DE GALLO

PUERTO ESCONDIDO, OAXACA, MEXICO

Sometimes referred to as the Mexican Pipeline, where giant sandbars cause these rugged waves to jack up in size. Now a fixture on the Big Wave Tour, this wave is gnarly, and even the paddle out can be a challenge.

I'll often pick up a burrito-style wrap when I'm on the move in the morning. Better still when they are made from cassava flour and are gluten free. Really it's all about convenience, so this is a handy option.

SERVES 2 - TOTAL TIME: 30 MIN

Ingredients for the pico de gallo:

1 plum tomato, diced
½ jalapeño, diced
¼ red onion, diced
¼ cup chopped cilantro
Juice of ½ lime
Sea salt and black pepper

Ingredients for the burrito:

1 tsp vegetable oil
4 oz fresh chorizo, removed from casing
½ cup cooked black beans with liquid
4 eggs
Sea salt and black pepper
Hot sauce
2 large, gluten-free tortillas
1 avocado, diced

FOR THE PICO DE GALLO, combine the tomato, jalapeño, onion, cilantro, and lime juice in a small bowl. Season with salt and pepper and mix.

FOR THE BURRITO, heat the vegetable oil in a large nonstick skillet over medium-high heat. Add the chorizo and break it up in the pan, cooking for about 5 minutes until slightly crispy. Remove meat from the skillet with a slotted spoon and place on a paper towel.

POUR THE BLACK BEANS and their liquid into a small saucepan and warm up over medium heat. Set aside.

BEAT THE EGGS well in a medium bowl. Season with salt and pepper and a decent splash of hot sauce. Pour the eggs into a clean skillet and cook over medium heat, stirring, for 5 minutes, until just set. Remove the eggs from the skillet and keep warm. Clean the skillet and return to the heat. Warm both sides of the tortillas, one at a time, in the skillet.

TO ASSEMBLE THE BURRITO. Lay a warm tortilla on a plate and layer on the scrambled egg, chorizo, black beans, and avocado, followed by a good spoonfull of pico de gallo. Then fold up one end of the tortilla, and then tightly roll in both sides, to prevent the contents falling out.

SERVE with additional pico de gallo and hot sauce.

DITCH PLAINS GREEN PANCAKES
WITH ONIONS, CHILI & SPINACH

DITCH PLAINS, MONTAUK, USA

One hundred twenty miles east of New York City, you arrive at the last town on the Long Island peninsula: Montauk. This spot can produce a 10-foot wave when the Atlantic Ocean's hurricane season kicks off.

My girls and I visit the Hamptons every year for a charity stand-up paddle event and to visit long-time friends in the area. These pancakes are light and are typical of the village cafés up and down that coast—but better still, they're loaded with iron-rich spinach, which helps make the hemoglobin in red blood cells that carry oxygen throughout our bodies.

SERVES 2 - TOTAL TIME: 30 MIN

Ingredients for the lemon butter:

¼ cup raw butter, softened
2 tsp grated lemon zest
1 tsp minced parsley
Sea salt and black pepper

Ingredients for the pancakes:

5 oz spinach leaves, washed
2 Tbsp raw butter, melted
3 green onions, finely sliced
1 jalapeño pepper, trimmed, seeded, and minced
½ cup gluten-free flour
¾ Tbsp baking powder
2 eggs
½ tsp ground cumin
⅓ cup almond milk
Sea salt and black pepper
Olive oil, for the pan
Lemon wedges, for garnish

FOR THE LEMON BUTTER, whisk together all the ingredients in a small bowl until blended. Place in the freezer to firm up while you prepare the pancakes.

FOR THE PANCAKES, preheat the oven to 200°F. Heat a little water in a small pan over medium heat. Add the spinach leaves, cover, and cook for just 1 minute, until the spinach wilts. Place the spinach in a bowl to cool down. Drain the spinach and coarsely chop. Combine the melted raw butter, green onions, jalapeño, and spinach in a mixing bowl. Add the flour, baking powder, eggs, cumin, and almond milk. Season with salt and pepper. Give it a good whisk to combine.

COAT A NONSTICK SKILLET over medium-high heat with olive oil. When the pan is hot, pour on several ¼-cup pancakes. Cook about 3 minutes, until air bubbles form on the surface, then flip them over and give the other sides a couple of minutes. Add a little more oil as the skillet dries out. You can stack the cooked pancakes on a plate and keep them warm in the oven until ready to serve.

TO SERVE, place the desired quantity of pancakes on a plate with a teaspoon of lemon butter on top and a lemon wedge on the side.

The hard work before the big pay off.

SHIMEI BAY OMELET WITH STIR-FRIED VEGETABLES IN SESAME OIL WITH NOODLES

SHIMEI BAY, HAINAN ISLAND, CHINA

Undoubtedly the capital of surfing along China's 9,000-mile coastline. This part of the island is sometimes referred to as China's Hawaii, and in the winter, this left break can get to a respectable size, perfect for long-boarding.

I grew up eating Chinese food because of its strong connection to Hawaii. I've always been fascinated with the unique techniques and cooking tools used. This spin on a classic omelet includes wok-fried vegetables, which take only a few minutes and are fabulously crunchy. If you want to avoid soy sauce, try balsamic vinegar or ponzu sauce as a replacement.

SERVES 2 - TOTAL TIME: 20 MIN

2 oz dried rice noodles

1 tsp toasted sesame oil

1 clove garlic, finely chopped

1 thumb of ginger, grated

10 asparagus tips

1 cup bean sprouts

1 cup carrot, shredded

1 tsp minced red chili

4 eggs

1 spring onion, chopped

Sea salt

1 tsp vegetable oil

1 tsp black and/or white
    sesame seeds

1 Tbsp chopped cilantro

Soy sauce, for serving

PREPARE THE NOODLES by placing in a heatproof bowl and covering with boiling water. Let stand for about 5 minutes, until tender, then drain.

FOR THE STIR-FRY, heat the sesame oil in a wok or large skillet over high heat, swirling the pan to coat. Add the garlic and ginger and stir-fry for 1 minute. Add the remaining vegetables and stir-fry for 3 minutes, or until the vegetables are tender. Transfer them to a bowl, add the noodles, and combine.

WHISK THE EGGS and stir in the chopped spring onion; season with salt. Heat the vegetable oil in a medium nonstick skillet over medium heat. Add half of the egg mixture and swirl to coat entire base of the pan. Cook for about 1 minute, or until eggs are set. Spread half of the vegetables over half the omelet; cook for 1 minute. Sprinkle with sesame seeds and cilantro and season with salt. Fold over to encase the filling. Repeat with the remaining eggs and filling.

TO SERVE, slide each omelet onto a plate and drizzle lightly with soy sauce.

NIJIMA MIXED MUSHROOM RAGOUT WITH POACHED EGG

NIJIMA, JAPAN

This island is about eight hours south of Tokyo by boat. It is truly a paradise surf destination, with clear blue water and white sandy beaches (though my lasting memory of the island was being stung by a giant sting ray).

Mushrooms of any variety may well be the ultimate superfood, because of the nutrients they absorb where they grow, but try and get hold of some Japanese varieties like shiitake. These are low in calories, but packed with B-complex vitamins that improve metabolism and the conversion of food into energy.

SERVES 2 - TOTAL TIME: 60 MIN

3 Tbsp olive oil

1 clove garlic, minced

½ medium onion, finely chopped

½ lb mixed fresh mushrooms, roughly chopped

Leaves from 2 sprigs thyme

Leaves from 1 stalk rosemary, chopped

Sea salt and black pepper

1 tsp gluten-free flour

¼ cup vegetable stock

1 tbsp chopped parsley

2 eggs

4 slices gluten-free bread, toasted

HEAT THE OLIVE OIL in a large skillet over medium-high heat. Add the garlic and onion. Cook until tender, about 5 minutes. Add the mushrooms, thyme, and rosemary and turn up the heat a little. Cook until the mushrooms start to sweat, then season with a pinch of salt. Sprinkle in the flour and cook, stirring, until the mushrooms are nice and soft, 5 minutes. Add the stock and let the liquid boil down a bit, leaving the mushrooms well glazed. Remove from heat and add the parsley. Season with salt and pepper if needed.

TO POACH THE EGGS, fill a small pan with enough water to submerge an egg in. Add a splash of vinegar and bring to a boil. Crack an egg into a small cup and gently pour into the water. Immediately remove the pan from the heat and set aside for 6 minutes. Drain.

TO SERVE, set 2 slices of toast on each plate and mound half of the mushroom ragout on top, then place a poached egg carefully in the center.

ANCHOR POINT SHAKSHUKA
WITH TOMATOES, PEPPERS, ARTICHOKES & SMOKED PAPRIKA WITH EGGS

ANCHOR POINT, TAGHAZOUT, MOROCCO

First ridden by the Australian surfers in the 1960s, this is probably Morocco's most famous spot. In the winter months between October and April, swells arrive from storms in the North Atlantic, thousands of miles away, producing a world-class, long, fast wave with plenty of horsepower—ideal conditions for foiling.

This shakshuka is at the apex of all-day eggs. It originated in North Africa, and the name means "mixture," so your choice of ingredients is open to interpretation. I've added local artichokes for their ability to lower blood cholesterol; they are also packed with antioxidants, making for a stronger defense system.

SERVES 4 - TOTAL TIME: 30 MIN

3 Tbsp olive oil

1 medium onion, sliced thin

1 red bell pepper, trimmed, seeded, sliced thin

1 red hot chili, trimmed, seeded, sliced thin

3 cloves garlic, crushed

1 ½ Tbsp smoked paprika

2 tsp ground cumin

1 (28-oz) can whole peeled tomatoes, crushed

Sea salt and black pepper

¼ cup chopped parsley

¼ cup chopped cilantro

4 eggs

½ cup pitted black olives

½ cup artichoke hearts

HEAT THE OLIVE OIL in a large, deep skillet over high heat. Add the onion, red pepper, and chili and spread them out evenly. Cook without disturbing until the vegetables start to soften, about 6 minutes. Stir them up and repeat to cook all sides, about 4 minutes. Add the garlic and cook until soft and fragrant, about 30 seconds. Stir in the paprika and cumin, followed by the tomatoes. Reduce the heat and simmer for about 10 minutes. Season to taste with salt and pepper, and stir in half of the parsley and cilantro.

USE A LARGE SPOON to make an egg-size well up against the edge of the pan and break an egg into it. Spoon some of the surrounding sauce over the egg white, keeping the yolk exposed. Repeat this process evenly around the pan, seasoning the eggs with salt as you go. Cook until the eggs are set but still runny, about 8 minutes.

TO SERVE, spoon out one full egg and some sauce onto each plate, sprinkle with the remaining parsley and cilantro. A slice of gluten-free bread on the side works really well.

ALEUTIAN WILD SALMON & QUINOA BURGER WITH PESTO & TWO EGGS

THE ALEUTIAN ISLANDS, ALASKA, USA

The last frontier, often referred to as "frozen Hawaii," the Aleutian Islands are on a similar longitude as Honolulu. But this type of surfing requires an expedition and some reasonable weather, so I choose to surf the snow instead, and visit annually with a group of friends for world-class heliboarding.

Wild Alaskan salmon is among the best in the world, and if you can find chinook or sockeye, both are highly prized for their rich flavor and firm texture, but also for containing more vitamin D than any other fish. These quinoa-encrusted burgers are another healthful, all-day breakfast.

SERVES 2 - TOTAL TIME: 30 MIN

Ingredients for the pesto (yields 4 cups):
- ¼ cup walnuts
- ¼ cup pine nuts
- 3 cloves garlic, chopped
- 5 cups basil
- 1 tsp sea salt
- 1 tsp black pepper
- 1 ½ cups extra-virgin olive oil
- 1 cup grated Parmesan cheese

Ingredients for the burgers:
- Olive oil, for the pan
- 10 oz wild salmon
- Sea salt and black pepper
- 2 green onions, chopped
- ¼ cup chopped flat-leaf parsley
- Grated zest of 1 lemon
- 1 egg, beaten
- 1 cup cooked quinoa
- 2 Tbsp olive oil
- 1 Tbsp butter, for the pan
- 4 eggs, fried sunny-side up

Preheat oven to 400°F.

THE PESTO IS THE MAGIC HERE. Place all the ingredients in a food processor fitted with a steel blade. Thoroughly purée the mixture and use right away.

FOR THE SALMON, lightly oil a baking tray. Season salmon steak with salt and pepper and bake on the middle rack of the oven, 20 minutes.

IN A LARGE MIXING BOWL, flake the cooked salmon with a fork. Mix in the onions, parsley, lemon zest, and egg. Use your hands to combine with the cooked quinoa. Season with salt and pepper to taste.

SHAPE THE SALMON mixture into four patties. Heat the olive oil in a large nonstick skillet over medium-high heat. Fry the patties for approximately 3 minutes on each side until crisp and golden.

MELT THE BUTTER in a large nonstick skillet over medium heat. Crack each egg onto the skillet and cook until the whites are just set and the yolks are still runny. Serve 2 eggs on each burger.

HALF MOON COFFEE & CACAO GRANOLA

WITH NATURAL YOGURT & ROASTED STRAWBERRIES

HALF MOON BAY, NORTHERN CALIFORNIA, USA

Located just south of the notorious Mavericks, where winter storms and a ramping rock formation can produce crests of over sixty feet high. Another deadly wave where conditions are hazardous, and the big boys lurk beneath the surface. A red triangle.

I was born twenty-five miles up the coast in San Francisco, where there are myriad amazing and creative granola manufacturers. There are so many healthy benefits, but the secret is to custom-make your own, so that it is right for your system. I love my coffee, so to gain the digestive advantages, and to get a kick out of it, adding an espresso charge works for me.

SERVES 4 - TOTAL TIME: 20 MIN

2 cups whole strawberries

½ cup raw honey

2 cups rolled oats

½ cup mixed raw nuts, chopped (walnuts, pecans, and almonds recommended)

¼ cup mixed seeds (pumpkin and sunflower recommended)

½ cup chopped unsweetened dried fruit

3 Tbsp Laird Superfood Cacao Creamer (optional)

1 Tbsp Laird Superfood Peruvian ground coffee

2 Tbsp coconut oil

½ tsp vanilla extract

Pinch of sea salt

2 cups natural plain yogurt

Preheat oven to 300°F.

TOSS THE STRAWBERRIES in raw honey and place on a baking tray. Roast for about 45 minutes.

IN A LARGE MIXING BOWL, combine all the other ingredients, using your hands to toss and coat. The coconut oil may start solid but will soon melt as you work the mix.

SPREAD THINLY on a large rimmed baking tray and bake for about 15 minutes, until browned and crispy. Let cool before serving or storing.

TO SERVE, spoon 1 cup granola into a small bowl. Top with a dollop of natural yogurt and some roasted strawberries.

You don't need a 30-foot wave to get your kicks!
Paddle-foil boarding at home in Hanalei Bay.

LES CAVALIERS SALMON, SPINACH & SUN-DRIED TOMATO CREPES

LES CAVALIERS, ANGLET, SW FRANCE

Just north of Biarritz and the mecca of French surf history there's an exposed beach break that can deliver all year-round. I spent the greater part of my career sponsored by a French company, and I hold vivid memories of the people and hospitality in this Northern Basque region. Savory or sweet, crêpes are definitively French. We use a gluten-free cassava flour recipe that works for your choice of filling. The intensely flavored sun-dried tomatoes provide a concentrated source of nutrients, including vitamins C and K, plus iron.

- **Ingredients for the crêpes:**

  7 Tbsp raw butter, melted,
  plus more for the pan

  1 cup almond milk

  1 cup gluten-free flour

  3 large eggs

  Pinch of sea salt

- **Ingredients for the sauce:**

  1 ½ Tbsp raw butter

  1 Tbsp gluten-free flour

  1 cup almond milk

  3 Tbsp fresh lemon juice

  Pinch of cayenne pepper

  Sea salt and black pepper

- **Ingredients for the filling:**

  1 Tbsp olive oil

  1 clove garlic, minced

  ½ cup spinach, trimmed

  2 Tbsp chopped sun-dried
  tomatoes

  ½ tsp fresh lemon juice

  Sea salt and black pepper

  2 (4-oz) boneless, skinless
  salmon fillets

  1 Tbsp grated Parmesan cheese
  (optional)

  2 Tbsp chopped chives,
  for garnish

Preheat the oven to 425°F with a rack in the middle. Grease an ovenproof dish with butter.

COMBINE THE MILK, FLOUR, EGGS, 5 tablespoons of the butter, and the salt in a blender. Blend to a smooth consistency. Decant the batter into a medium bowl.

SET A MEDIUM NONSTICK SKILLET over medium heat and coat the bottom with some of the remaining melted butter. Ladle ¼ cup of the batter into the center of the pan and rotate, swirling the mixture evenly around the bottom of the pan. Cook for about 1 minute, until the underside of the crêpe is golden brown. Carefully turn the crêpe over and cook for another 30 seconds or until cooked. Repeat this process, stacking the crêpes on a covered plate.

FOR THE SAUCE, melt the butter in a small saucepan over medium heat. Add the flour and stir until smooth, about 1 minute. Pour in the milk, stirring constantly; the mixture will start to thicken. Cook for 1 minute, remove from heat, then add the lemon juice and cayenne and stir until blended. Season with salt and pepper.

FOR THE FILLING, heat the oil in a medium, ovenproof skillet over medium heat; add the garlic and cook, stirring, for 2 minutes, until light brown. Drop in the spinach and stir until coated and completely wilted. Turn off the heat and add the sun-dried tomatoes and lemon juice. Season with salt and pepper.

ARRANGE A CREPE on a cutting board, placing one piece of the salmon down first; spoon half the spinach mix over the top, fold up both sides of the crêpes tightly and place in the prepared pan. Repeat with another crêpe. Spoon the sauce evenly over the top of both and grate some Parmesan over the top. Cook for 20 minutes until bubbling and golden. Sprinkle with chives and serve.

CHESTERMAN GLUTEN-FREE TOAST, BACON, ROASTED CHERRY TOMATOES & GUACAMOLE

CHESTERMAN BEACH, BRITISH COLUMBIA, CANADA

Set among the stunning islands of British Columbia, this beach break on Tofino Peninsula, a favorite among the locals, is unbeatable for stand-up paddle touring. My thrills, however, have once again been on my snowboard, close by in Whistler, bombing the Black Hole double-black run.

As if we need a reason to eat bacon (and there are plenty)! Bacon is loaded with an important macronutrient called choline, which works in a similar way to vitamin B—great for brain function and memory retention.

SERVES 2 - TOTAL TIME: 30 MIN

8 strips of bacon

12 cherry tomatoes, halved

2 ripe avocadoes, diced

¼ red onion, diced

1 clove garlic, crushed

½ red hot chili, trimmed
   and seeded, minced

2 Tbsp chopped cilantro

1 Tbsp fresh lime juice

Sea salt and black pepper

4 slices gluten-free toast

Preheat oven to 400°F. Line an oven tray with foil.

PLACE THE BACON strips side by side on the oven tray; arrange the tomato halves cut sides up next to the bacon. Cook for about 25 minutes, until the bacon begins to crisp and the tomatoes reduce in size and shrivel at the edges.

MEANWHILE, MAKE THE GUACAMOLE.

In a medium bowl, combine the avocado, onion, garlic, chili pepper, cilantro, and lime juice; season with salt and pepper. Mash thoroughly with a fork.

ARRANGE THE TOAST on two plates and divide up the bacon between them. Top with a generous spoonful of guacamole and a few roasted tomatoes.

LAIRD'S BANANA & TURMERIC SMOOTHIE

SERVES 2 - TOTAL TIME: 5 MIN

2 bananas

1 cup pineapple chunks

½ inch fresh ginger, grated

½ cup almond milk

Juice of 1 lime

2 Tbsp hemp seeds

1 Tbsp Laird Superfood
Turmeric Creamer

(or 1 tsp ground turmeric)

½ tsp ground cinnamon

1 ½ tsp local honey

½ tsp vanilla extract

8 ice cubes

Fresh turmeric, grated,
   for garnish

Almond, grated, for garnish

COMBINE all the ingredients except the turmeric and almond in a blender and process until smooth and aerated, adding more almond milk if necessary. Garnish with grated turmeric and almond.

LAIRD'S BEET & BERRY SMOOTHIE

SERVES 2 - TOTAL TIME: 5 MIN

1 ½ cups almond milk

2 Tbsp Laird Superfood
   creamer

2 Tbsp chia seeds

2 Tbsp cashew butter

2 cups fresh spinach

1 banana

1 cup raspberries

½ cup strawberries

½ cup cubed beets

4 ice cubes

COMBINE all the ingredients in a blender and process until smooth and aerated, adding a little more almond milk if necessary.

LAIRD'S LEAN GREEN SMOOTHIE

SERVES 2 - TOTAL TIME: 5 MIN

1 cup kale leaves, chopped

1 cup spinach, chopped

2 Tbsp Original Laird Superfood Creamer (optional)

½ cup green grapes

1 large apple, chopped

1 avocado, chopped

1 Tbsp raw meal powder

4 ice cubes

Apple juice or water, as needed

COMBINE all the ingredients in a blender and process until smooth and aerated, adding a little apple juice or water if necessary.

LAIRD'S COFFEE & CACAO SMOOTHIE

SERVES 2 - TOTAL TIME: 5 MIN

2 shots espresso coffee

1 banana

¼ cup rolled oats

2 Tbsp Laird Superfood Cacao Creamer (or cacao powder)

2 Tbsp flaxseed meal

⅛ tsp ground cinnamon

1 cup almond milk

1 tsp local honey

4 ice cubes

COMBINE all the ingredients in a blender and process until smooth and aerated, adding a little more almond milk if necessary.

SECOND SESSION

A bit of adrenaline each day keeps boredom at bay,
and I have always loved launching into the ocean from the cliffs.

MUNDAKA TOMATO, CARROT & TURMERIC BISQUE SOUP

MUNDAKA, PAIS VASCO, SPAIN

I was last here about ten years ago, stand-up surfing close by at Roca Puta. This is a world-class gem, the left wave breaking over a river-mouth sandbar, creating long, fast, barreling rides.

The Basque region in Spain is rich with incredible cooking, and this simple soup could not get any better. Tomatoes are often considered a vegetable, but in fact they are a fruit. One of its many benefits is a substance called lycopene, which can help prevent cancer.

SERVES 4–6 TOTAL TIME: 1 HR

6 large tomatoes
1 onion, chopped
1 carrot, chopped
4 Tbsp raw butter
3 Tbsp gluten-free flour
1 quart organic chicken broth
1 clove garlic, crushed
3 green onions, chopped
Sea salt and black pepper
1 cup water
2 Tbsp Laird Superfood
Turmeric Creamer
   (or 2 tsp ground turmeric)
10 chives, chopped, for garnish
Gluten-free croutons,
   for garnish

BRING A LARGE POT OF WATER TO A BOIL.

Cut an 'X' in the bottom of each tomato, and place them in the boiling water for 1 minute, until the skins begin to split. Lift out with slotted spoon and plunge into cold water. Peel off the skins, halve the tomatoes, scoop out the seeds, and chop.

IN A LARGE, DEEP PAN, sauté the onion and carrot in the butter until the onion begins to color. Add flour and mix well. Slowly add the broth, tomatoes, garlic, and green onions. Season with salt and pepper. Cover, and cook over low heat for 1 hour.

PURÉE IN BLENDER, add 1 cup water and the Laird Superfood Turmeric Creamer, and process again. Serve garnished with chives and gluten-free croutons. Season to taste with salt and pepper.

MARINARETTI ZUCCHINI SOUP

MARINARETTI, PORT ANZIO, ITALY

I haven't visited this particular spot, although we did hunt some waves while filming *Point Break 2* in the area. My lasting memory of Italy? Paddling with Buzzy Kerbox from Corsica across to Isola d'Elba, some forty miles of misery.

This is a simple, classic Italian soup. The great thing about zucchini is that it is extremely low in calories, so you can fill up your stomach without the consequences. Studies have shown that this fruit has properties that can help treat symptoms of benign prostatic hypertrophy.

SERVES 4–6 TOTAL TIME: 30 MIN

3 medium zucchinis, trimmed

2 Tbsp extra-virgin olive oil

2 cloves garlic, crushed

Sea salt and black pepper

2 cups organic chicken broth

1 bunch basil, chopped

1 bunch flat-leaf parsley, chopped

4 oz Parmesan cheese, grated, plus more for serving (optional)

½ cup water

2 Tbsp Laird Superfood Unsweetened Creamer

Gluten-free toast, for serving

CUT THE ZUCCHINI lengthwise into quarters, then into 1-inch pieces. Heat the oil in a heavy saucepan over medium heat. Add the zucchini and garlic and cook for 25 minutes, until the zucchini are soft and starting to brown. Season with salt and pepper. Add the broth and simmer for another few minutes.

POUR THE SOUP into a blender. Add the basil, parsley, and Parmesan and blend. Return the soup to the pan and add the water and Laird Superfood Unsweetened Creamer.

SERVE with some gluten-free toast and additional grated Parmesan.

MULLAGHMORE BEET & APPLE SOUP

MULLAGHMORE, COUNTY DONEGAL, IRELAND

On Ireland's remote northwest shores, this is an extremely heavy wave and not for the wary. You'll need a thick wetsuit and thicker skin, and be ready to get washed on the rocks. Beets are a prehistoric food originally grown for its leaves; it wasn't cultivated as a root vegetable until Roman times. Although they have a higher sugar content than any other vegetable, the powerful benefits are undeniable: Consuming beets can reduce blood pressure in a matter of hours, a result of the nitrates contained in the beets converting to nitric oxide, which in turn helps dilate your blood vessels.

SERVES 4–6 TOTAL TIME: 40 MIN

1 large onion, chopped

1 Tbsp olive oil

4 large beets, cooked, peeled, and chopped

1 large apple, peeled, cored, and chopped

3 cups vegetable broth

1 Tbsp chopped fresh dill

Sea salt and black pepper

1 tsp apple cider vinegar

2 Tbsp Original Laird Superfood Creamer

4-6 sprigs fresh dill, for garnish

IN A LARGE, DEEP PAN, sauté the onion in the oil until softened and translucent. Add the beets and the apple and cook for 5 minutes.

ADD THE BROTH and dill to the pan and season with salt and pepper. Simmer, covered, for 15 minutes, until the apple and beets are tender.

PUT THE SOUP in a blender and blend until smooth. Stir in the vinegar and the Laird Superfood Creamer and return to the pan to warm through.

SERVE GARNISHED with a sprig of fresh dill.

HANALEI BOWL CHILLED AVOCADO SOUP WITH SUMMER SALSA

THE BOWL, HANALEI BAY, KAUAI

My backyard for six months out of the year. Named for the curved shape of the wave resembling a large bowl (see image on pages 6-7). When it's big, you'll pay if you get caught on the inside here. This is just one of the seventeen named surf spots found in the bay. Technically, the avocado is a berry. I have several large trees on my land in Hawaii, and they satisfy my needs comfortably throughout the year. They are more popular than ever right now because they contain nearly twenty vitamins and minerals, including potassium, which helps control blood pressure. They are also low in sugar and high in fiber, helping you to feel full for longer.

SERVES 4–6 TOTAL TIME: 30 MIN

Ingredients for the soup:

4 ripe avocados (Haas), peeled, pitted, and chopped

1 quart organic vegetable broth

¼ cup fresh lemon juice

Sea salt

Splash of extra-virgin olive oil, for serving

Ingredients for the salsa:

½ small red onion, chopped

10 cherry tomatoes, chopped

3 Tbsp chopped cilantro

½ yellow bell pepper, diced

½ cup cucumber, diced

1 red hot chili, trimmed, seeded, and finely chopped

2 Tbsp extra-virgin olive oil

2 tsp fresh lemon juice

Sea salt

PUT THE AVOCADOS in a blender along with the broth and lemon juice and blend at high speed for 1 minute, until really smooth.

Season with salt and pour into an airtight container. Chill for at least 30 minutes.

FOR THE SALSA, combine all the ingredients in a small bowl and season with salt.

TO SERVE, pour the soup into bowls and top with a few generous spoonfuls of salsa. Drizzle some olive oil over the top. Serve within a couple of hours to ensure the soup remains a bright color.

PLAYA GRANDE GRILLED PORK BURGER
WITH CHIMICHURRI SAUCE & SWEET POTATO FRIES

PLAYA GRANDE, MAR DEL PLATA, ARGENTINA

Found at the northeast corner of Argentina's 300-mile coastline, this city is surf central. The best swell is in the winter months, but be prepared: It comes up from the Antarctic. I take the scenic option, and head up into the Andes in Patagonia for breathtaking hiking and unparalleled heliboarding. This chimichurri is similar to a European pesto, and can be brushed and basted onto the meat during cooking or served as an accompaniment.

SERVES 4 - TOTAL TIME: 45 MIN

Ingredients for the chimichurri:

1 cup chopped flat-leaf parsley
½ cup extra-virgin olive oil
⅓ cup red wine vinegar
¼ cup chopped cilantro
2 cloves garlic
¾ tsp red pepper flakes
½ tsp ground cumin
½ tsp sea salt

Ingredients for the burgers:

3 Tbsp olive oil, additional for grilling
½ cup diced shallots
1 ½ tsp ground cumin
3 cloves garlic, minced
1 Tbsp thyme leaves
2 chiles de arbol, finely sliced
Sea salt and black pepper
30 oz ground pork
4 oz chorizo, removed from casing
3 oz smoked bacon, finely sliced
2 Tbsp chopped parsley

Ingredients for sweet potato fries:

4 medium sweet potatoes

Preheat the oven to 400°F.

FOR THE CHIMICHURRI, combine all the ingredients in a food processor.

FOR THE BURGERS, heat the oil in a medium skillet over medium heat. Add the shallots and stir until they soften. Add the cumin, garlic, thyme, and chiles. Season with salt and pepper. Cook for another 5 minutes, then set aside to cool.

IN A LARGE MIXING BOWL, use your hands to combine the pork, chorizo, bacon, parsley, and the cooled shallot mixture. Shape the mixture into eight patties, and refrigerate until ready to cook.

HEAT A CHARCOAL GRILL or a ridged grill pan (a BBQ is always more fun and adds to the flavor). Brush the patties with olive oil before cooking. Cook for about 4 minutes per side, until just cooked through.

PEEL THE POTATOES and slice into half-inch fries. Toss in olive oil and roast on an oven tray at 400°F for 45 minutes, turning over halfway through cooking.

SERVE WITH HAND-CUT, roasted sweet potato fries and chimichurri on the side.

Off on another adventure with photography legend Don King and tow partner Terry Chung.

CLOUDBREAK SEARED TUNA WITH CRUNCHY SALAD WITH RED POTATOES & LEMON

CLOUDBREAK, TAVARUA, FIJI

Now we're talking my top five in the world. An absolutely perfect-looking left reef pass that is also one of the most challenging waves to surf. It gets serious here very quickly, and proximity to the razor-sharp coral reef makes wipeouts worth avoiding. Cloudbreak's position on the edge of the Mamanuca archipelago means that premium-grade fish are in abundance. When you buy fresh tuna to prepare in this way, be sure the meat looks pale pink or reddish, has been recently cut, appears moist, and smells fresh. If in any doubt, ask the vendor for a fresh cut.

SERVES 4 - TOTAL TIME: 20 MIN

Ingredients for the tuna:

1 Tbsp coriander seeds
1 tsp red pepper flakes
½ cup finely chopped cilantro
½ clove garlic, minced
½ cup finely chopped basil
Juice of 1 lemon
Sea salt and black pepper
4 (8-oz) tuna steaks, ¾ in thick
Olive oil, for cooking

Ingredients for the salad:

1 cucumber, sliced
1 head iceberg lettuce, roughly chopped
½ cup black olives, pitted and sliced
6 oz sun-dried tomatoes or roasted
    red peppers, drained and sliced
10 small red potatoes, boiled and halved
1 lemon, quartered

CRUSH the coriander seeds thoroughly with a mortar and pestle. Mix in a small bowl with the red pepper flakes, cilantro, garlic, basil, and lemon juice. Season with salt and pepper. Coat both sides of the tuna steaks with the mixture.

TO COOK, coat a medium ridged skillet with olive oil and place over high heat. When the pan is smoking hot, put in the tuna and cook for just 1 minute on each side; this really sears the crust on the outside while the middle stays beautifully pink.

TO PREPARE the salad, divide the ingredients among four large bowls, then break up the tuna steaks by hand into a few pieces and lay on top. Serve with a wedge of lemon on the side.

UCHIUMI POINT STEAK SALAD WITH EDAMAME, GREENS & ORANGE SESAME DRESSING

UCHIUMI, KYUSHU, JAPAN

An exposed reef break found on the most southwesterly of Japan's four main islands. In typhoon season this can really come alive, but it is shallow—and beware of sea urchins. Just close by is Curren's Point, named after legendary world-champion surfer Tom Curren from Santa Barbara.

This is one of Gabby's favorite salads to make; we have prepared it with various types of meat. Undoubtedly, if you have access to some genuine Kobe beef from Japan, you are in for a real treat, as it's world-renowned for its flavor and tenderness.

SERVES 2 - TOTAL TIME: 20 MIN

Ingredients for the salad:

1 cup shelled edamame beans
½ cup thinly sliced cabbage
½ cup Asian greens
3 green onions (white parts), finely sliced
1 red bell pepper, trimmed, seeded, and sliced
10 cherry tomatoes, halved
3 Tbsp toasted sesame oil
2 tri-tip steaks, thinly sliced

Ingredients for the dressing:

¼ cup fresh orange juice
¼ cup rice vinegar
2 Tbsp soy sauce
1 Tbsp local honey
1 Tbsp toasted sesame oil
1 tsp grated fresh ginger

FOR THE DRESSING, combine ingredients in a small bowl.

FOR THE SALAD, toss the edamame, cabbage, greens, onions, peppers, and tomatoes in a medium bowl.

HEAT THE SESAME OIL in a medium skillet over high heat. Add the steak strips and cook to your liking, about 1 minute for medium.

WHEN SLIGHTLY COOLED, add the steak to the salad, pour the dressing over it, and turn over once. Serve in large salad bowls.

FIRST POINT GRILLED TILAPIA TACOS WITH KIWI, POMEGRANATE & LIME SALSA WITH GLUTEN-FREE TORTILLAS

FIRST POINT, MALIBU, CALIFORNIA, USA

My backyard "wave machine" for the summertime. This world-famous right-hand point break is a crowded spot. My highlight riding here was when Hurricane Marie was hammering California in August 2014. I stand-up paddle-surfed from dawn until dusk, shooting the Malibu Pier several times.

We use cassava flour to make homemade gluten-free tortillas, but you can buy gluten-free ones at the store. The family likes to get creative with accompaniments to their fish tacos, and this fruit salsa is the bomb! Original, fresh, light, and easy.

SERVES 2 - TOTAL TIME 20 MIN

Ingredients for the salsa:
4 kiwis, peeled and chopped
¼ cup pomegranate seeds
½ avocado, diced
2 green onions
   (white parts), sliced
1 fresh jalapeño, trimmed,
   seeded, and chopped fine
1 Tbsp chopped cilantro
1 tsp extra-virgin olive oil
Sea salt and black pepper

Ingredients for the tacos:
Sea salt and black pepper
1 tilapia (or white fish) fillet,
   halved
1 Tbsp olive oil
4 medium gluten-free tortillas,
   warmed

PREPARE THE SALSA: Combine all the ingredients in a medium bowl and mix togther. Season with salt and pepper.

SEASON THE FISH FILLET and cut into four pieces. Heat a ridged skillet over medium-high heat. Coat in olive oil and grill the fish for 2 to 3 minutes on each side, until marked and cooked through.

TO ASSEMBLE, place two tortillas on each plate and place a single piece of fish in the middle of each. Cover generously with two piled spoonfuls of the salsa; fold tortillas over filling.

IMSOUANE BAY SPICY SHRIMP WITH ORANGE

& SEASONAL QUINOA SALAD

IMSOUANE BAY, ESSAOUIRA, MOROCCO

One of the longest right-handers in Africa, perfect for foil-surfing, promising a ride of nearly half a mile long. Definitely on my radar in the near future. The backdrop is a bustling fishing community, with fleets of bright blue boats returning daily to take their catch to the fish-trading hall.

SERVES 2 - TOTAL TIME: 30 MIN

Ingredients for the shrimp:

1 Tbsp fresh rosemary,
   finely chopped

2 cloves garlic, crushed

3 Tbsp olive oil

1 tsp smoked paprika

1 thread saffron

12 large shrimp, cleaned,
   with the shells on

1 orange, cut into 8 wedges

Ingredients for quinoa salad:

2 cups cooked red quinoa

4 spears asparagus, sliced short

1 yellow bell pepper, trimmed,
   seeded, and diced small

1 red bell pepper, trimmed,
   seeded, and diced small

2 green onions (white parts), sliced

1 zucchini, diced small

½ cup pomegranate seeds

½ cup fresh mint finely sliced

Juice of 1 lemon

COMBINE THE ROSEMARY, garlic, oil, and spices in a medium bowl. Add the shrimp and orange and coat evenly in the mixture. Set aside.

FOR THE SALAD, fluff the cooled quinoa with a fork. Combine the quinoa and the salad ingredients in a large bowl, and season with salt and pepper.

COOK THE SHRIMP: Heat a large nonstick skillet over high heat. When the pan is smoking hot, pour in the shrimp, oranges, and marinade mixture. Cook for about 2 minutes on each side, until the shrimp start to brown and the oranges are partially caramelized.

TO SERVE, plate the quinoa salad and arrange the shrimp and the oranges on top. The oranges are great squeezed over the shrimp.

When you have the opportunity to buy large, fresh, shell-on shrimp, that's the time for this recipe. The combination of the sautéed oranges with the depth of the smoked paprika make this feel like North Africa.

66

Full speed ahead! The reduced friction from the foil makes for a fast ride.

KALO NERO GRILLED FIG & PROSCIUTTO SALAD

KALO NERO, PELOPONNISOS, GREECE

If you find yourself here in wintertime and with a decent offshore wind, you could see some action (though there are probably more convenient spots). My genuine interest in Greece is that my father was one hundred percent Greek, and that keeps me curious and fascinated by the national culture.

The fig is among the oldest fruits eaten by humans, and they have featured heavily in religious symbolism throughout time. One of my favorite facts is that ancient Olympians were awarded figs in recognition of their athletic achievements. Nutritionally, they boast an extremely high concentration of fiber, which helps regulate digestion.

SERVES 4 - TOTAL TIME: 35 MIN

Ingredients for the dressing:

1 Tbsp Dijon mustard

3 Tbsp red wine vinegar

1 tsp raw honey

½ cup extra-virgin olive oil

Sea salt and black pepper

Ingredients for salad:

4 cups halved figs

2 Tbsp raw butter, melted

1 tsp ground cinnamon

8 oz arugula

8 oz frisée

3 oz prosciutto, thinly sliced

8 oz goat cheese

⅓ cup shelled pistachios

2 tsp fresh thyme leaves

Sea salt and black pepper

Preheat the oven to 425°F.

FOR THE DRESSSING, in a small jar with a tight-fitting lid, combine the mustard, vinegar, and honey. Put the lid on and give it a good shake. Add the olive oil and shake for another 15 seconds; add salt and pepper to taste.

FOR THE FIG SALAD, place the halved figs cut sides up on a nonstick baking sheet. Drizzle the melted butter evenly over the figs, then lightly sprinkle the cinnamon over the top. Roast in the oven for about 10 minutes, until the figs become softened. Set aside to cool.

TO SERVE, arrange the arugula and frisée on serving plates and pour on a little dressing. Place the roasted figs cut sides up on the salad. Tear the prosciutto into strips and lay them over the top, then crumble on the goat cheese. Sprinkle the pistachios and thyme over the top. Season with salt and pepper.

We are lucky enough to have a lifetime supply
of coconuts on our property—a rewarding way to rehydrate.

IPANEMA FRESH VEGETABLE & COCONUT CURRY WITH WILD RICE

IPANEMA, RIO DE JANEIRO, BRAZIL

With four and a half thousand miles of Atlantic coastline, Brazil has a lot to offer surfers. Home to the biggest professional names in the sport, surf culture is on the ascension here. There are several beach breaks, right and left, on this popular beach. But beware the crowds and some intense locals.

This traditional vegetarian curry has a very different consistency from an Asian curry; it's distinctive because of the roasted vegetables, which make for real flavor. The eggplant is the hero here, as it's rich in antioxidants, specifically nasunin, found in the the skin, a free radical scavenger that protects the fats in your brain-cell membranes.

SERVES 4 - TOTAL TIME: 30 MIN

1 butternut squash, peeled
    and cut into 1-inch cubes
1 eggplant, chopped
2 red bell peppers, diced
3 Tbsp olive oil
1 red chili pepper, trimmed,
    seeded, and minced
2 cloves garlic, crushed
½ inch ginger root,
    peeled and chopped
1 red onion, chopped
1 (15-oz) can chopped tomatoes
1 cup coconut cream
1 (15-oz) can chickpeas
2 cups cooked wild rice
Sea salt and black pepper
¼ cup chopped cilantro,
    for garnish

Preheat the oven to 400°F.

SCATTER THE SQUASH, eggplant, and peppers on a rimmed, nonstick baking tray and coat with olive oil. Roast for 40 minutes.

PLACE THE CHILI, garlic, ginger, and onion in a food processor and blend to a course paste. Then heat the remaining oil in a skillet and sauté the paste until the mixture has softened. Add the tomatoes and simmer on medium heat for 10 minutes. Stir in the coconut cream and continue to simmer for 5 minutes.

ADD THE ROASTED VEGETABLES and the chickpeas to the sauce and heat through. Season with salt and pepper to taste.

SERVE WITH WILD RICE and garnish with cilantro.

RAGLAN QUINOA SALAD WITH GRILLED CORN, MANGO, TOMATOES, AVOCADO & GOAT CHEESE

RAGLAN, NORTH ISLAND, NEW ZEALAND

One of my favorites for tow-in foiling. Manu Bay, south of Raglan, has one of the longest and most consistent left breaks in the world, and with a foil you have the potential to ride for over a mile. This wave was also made famous by the classic surf film, *Endless Summer*. The life in this salad comes from the mango, a simple fruit that is actually in the same family as the cashew and pistachio, and is packed with powerful antioxidants that help neutralize free radicals, which cause degenerative diseases.

SERVES 4 - TOTAL TIME: 15 MIN

Ingredients for the dressing:

⅓ cup extra-virgin olive oil

2 Tbsp fresh lime juice

1 clove garlic, crushed

Sea salt and black pepper

Ingredients for the salad:

1 cup cooked quinoa

1 fresh mango, cubed

1 large avocado, cubed

15 cherry tomatoes, quartered

½ cup chopped mint

½ cup chopped cilantro

1 corn cob, boiled or grilled

5 chives, chopped

2 Tbsp goat cheese, crumbled

FOR THE DRESSSING, in a small jar with a tight-fitting lid, combine the olive oil, lime juice, and garlic; add salt and pepper to taste. Put the lid on the jar and give it a good shake.

FOR THE SALAD, fluff the cooled quinoa with a fork and place in a large bowl. Gently combine with the mango, avocado, tomatoes, mint, and cilantro. Slice the cooled corn off the cob into the salad, adding the chives and crumbling the goat cheese over the top.

SERVE in small bowls with lime dressing on the side.

SUPERBANK CHOPPED CHICKEN, BACON, EGG, SPINACH

& KALE SALAD, ASIAN PEAR, AVOCADO, CASHEW & RAISINS WITH CURRY DRESSING

SUPERBANK, GOLD COAST, AUSTRALIA

An epic must-visit for an experienced surfer, Superbank features on the professional world surfing tour. Interestingly, this is actually a man-made phenomenon, occurring when dredging more than six hundred thousand square feet of sand at the mouth of the Tweed River gave rise to cylinder-perfect barrels.

This chopped salad is equally perfect and fully loaded, all tied together by a distinctive curry dressing. The walnuts though, are the gold—consumption promotes brain function due to the omega-3 fatty acids, together with iodine and selenium, which stimulate brain activity.

SERVES 4 - TOTAL TIME: 30 MIN

Ingredients for the dressing:

⅓ cup extra-virgin olive oil

2 Tbsp fresh lemon juice

1 tsp curry powder

1 tsp Dijon mustard

Sea salt and black pepper

Ingredients for the salad:

4 eggs

Sea salt

1 precooked roast chicken, shredded

16 oz smoked bacon, chopped

2 Asian pears, julienned

2 avocados, cubed

1 cup unsalted roasted cashews

½ cup walnuts

½ cup raisins

2 cups packed chopped kale

2 cups packed chopped spinach

FOR THE DRESSSING, in a small jar with a tight-fitting lid, combine the olive oil, lemon juice, curry powder, and mustard; add salt and pepper to taste. Put the lid on the jar and give it a good shake.

BRING A SMALL PAN of water to a boil; add a little salt. Prick the bottom of each egg with an egg pricker and boil eggs for exactly 4 ½ minutes. Remove and immerse in cold water.

IN A LARGE MIXING BOWL combine all of the salad ingredients, except the eggs. Gently combine using salad tongs.

TO SERVE pile the salad mix in a large salad bowl. Crack and peel the eggs, and cut them over the salad; the soft yolks should just hold together. Drizzle with curry dressing.

PAPARA MARINATED SQUID WITH CHILI OIL & FRESH ROSEMARY SERVED ON ARUGULA SALAD

PAPARA, TAHITI, FRENCH POLYNESIA

Far less well-known than Teahupo'o, my number-two all-time wave, Papara is an uncrowded, exposed reef break off the largest island in French Polynesia. Tahiti is widely regarded as a tropical wave factory, but this locals' wave is right in front of my dear friend and legendary waterman Raimana Van Bastolaer's house.

Squid, often referred to by its Latin name, calamari, is packed with protein and low in calories and fat. Squid also provides trace minerals and nutrients that protect your heart, regulate your blood pressure, and balance your cholesterol.

SERVES 4 - TOTAL TIME: 20 MIN

10 oz fresh or frozen squid, washed and dried

4 cloves garlic, crushed

1 red chili, trimmed, seeded, and minced

3 Tbsp olive oil

Leaves from 2 rosemary sprigs, finely chopped

4 cups arugula (packed)

2 Tbsp fresh lemon juice

Sea salt

Gluten-free bread, for serving (optional)

CUT THE SQUID into very thin rings, keeping the tentacles whole. Put in a small bowl and add the garlic, chili, olive oil, and rosemary. Mix well and refrigerate for at least 1 hour.

HEAT A LARGE NONSTICK SKILLET until smoking hot, then add the squid and marinade. Cook, stirring, for no more than 1 minute, just until the flesh turns white; if you cook it longer, the squid becomes very rubbery.

TO SERVE toss the arugula in a light coating of lemon juice. Place it on the plate and top with a serving of squid, being sure to include some of the cooked marinade.

A SLICE OF GLUTEN-FREE BREAD is a great way to soak up the juices left on the plate.

Balance is one of the keys to a happy life, and to
practice its literal application is critical to my sport.

THIRD SESSION

WAIMEA AHI POKE WITH SWEET ONION, AVOCADO, SEAWEED & SESAME WITH WILD RICE

WAIMEA, OAHU, HAWAII

This surf spot is located on the legendary North Shore of Oahu. Waimea played a big role in the origin of big-wave surfing and is famous for the Eddie Aikau event that is held only when it's breaking above thirty-foot faces. In twenty-four years, this competition has only been run eight times. Meanwhile, summers there are absolutely flat, and you'd never believe a wave was possible!

The word "poke" means "chunk" in Hawaiian. This raw tuna salad isn't a new idea, but seems to be everywhere right now. There are no rules on the ingredients or size. In fact, if you are on the move, it is super convenient to throw it in a gluten-free wrap.

SERVES 4–6 TOTAL TIME: 15 MIN

2 oz dried seaweed

12 oz raw sashimi-grade tuna, cubed

3 oz sweet onion, finely diced

1 tsp mix of black and white sesame seeds

4 tsp soy sauce

2 tsp toasted sesame oil

1 tsp local honey

1 tsp red pepper flakes

Sea salt

1 cup cooked wild rice, cooled (optional)

REHYDRATE THE SEAWEED according to the package instructions. Drain it and cut it into thin slices.

COMBINE THE TUNA, onion, sesame seeds, soy sauce, sesame oil, honey, and red pepper flakes in a medium mixing bowl. Season with salt and gently toss. If you are serving this as a main course, stir in the cooled rice at this point. Toss again.

SERVE in small bowls with the seaweed on top.

POINT VENUS COCONUT CURRIED MUSSELS WITH LIME & GARLIC

POINT VENUS, TAHITI

The northernmost tip of Tahiti, where Captain Cook tracked the planet Venus in 1769. Similar to Papara, this is another exposed right-hand reef break. It's certainly just as hazardous, with sharp coral, large rocks, and an abundance of black tips. Tahitian cuisine is among the best, blending French and Asian influences. Cooked in a delicious curry broth, these mussels have an impressive nutritional profile. They contain some valuable fatty acids that offer great rewards, improving brain function and reducing inflamatory conditions such as arthritis.

SERVES 2 - TOTAL TIME: 40 MINS

1 stalk lemongrass,
   roughly chopped

3 Tbsp olive oil

1 yellow onion, sliced

3 cloves garlic

3 Tbsp grated fresh ginger

¼ cup green curry paste

1 (15-oz) can coconut milk

2 Tbsp fish sauce

¼ cup water

3 lb mussels, rinsed

2 limes, halved

½ cup chopped cilantro,
   for garnish

PREPARE THE LEMONGRASS: Cut off and retain the first 6 inches from the white, root end (discard the rest). Strip away the coarse outer layers to reveal the softer center. Roughly chop.

HEAT THE OLIVE OIL in a large, deep pot over medium-high heat. Add the onion and stir until softened. Add the garlic, lemongrass, ginger, and curry paste and cook, stirring, for 5 minutes. Add the coconut milk, fish sauce, and water and bring to a steady simmer.

ADD THE MUSSELS to the pot and cover. Simmer for 8 minutes, stirring occasionally. Throw away any shells that did not open.

TO SERVE, divide between bowls, squeeze limes over the top. and add the lime halves to the bowl. Sprinkle the cilantro to garnish.

LA TORCHE ROASTED CHICKEN

WITH LEMON, ROSEMARY, SAUTEED BRUSSELS SPROUTS & SMASHED CELERY ROOT

LA TORCHE, BRITTANY, NORTHWEST FRANCE

This battered promontory hosts the full gamut of water sports. Most memorably, I recall it as an international windsurfing hub. Radical Atlantic winds work best in the winter, but there are some wicked currents here, and local knowledge of how to use them is essential. Poulet rôti is as good as it gets! Preferably whole, as eating chicken from the bone is a special experience. The celery root, also know as celeriac, is not actually the root of the celery stalks that we know, although it shares the same taste.

SERVES 4 - TOTAL TIME: 135 MIN

Ingredients for the chicken:
1 (5-lb) free-range chicken
Sea salt and black pepper
1 lemon, halved
2 rosemary sprigs
Olive oil

Ingredients for the Brussels sprouts:
Sea salt and black pepper
10 oz Brussels sprouts, halved
3 Tbsp olive oil
2 oz pancetta, cubed
2 cloves garlic, minced
1 tsp minced red hot chili

Ingredients for the celery root:
3 Tbsp olive oil
2 cloves garlic, minced
1 tsp red pepper flakes
2 tsp thyme leaves
2 medium celery roots, peeled and cubed
2 cups organic chicken stock
Sea salt and black pepper

Preheat the oven to 375°F.

SEASON the inner cavity of the chicken with salt and pepper, then stuff with the lemon halves and rosemary. Evenly coat the skin all over with olive oil, and season with salt and pepper. Lay the chicken breast side up in a roasting pan and place on a high shelf in the oven. Cook for about 120 minutes, basting regularly, until a thermometer inserted reads 165°F. Let the chicken relax for at least 15 minutes before carving.

MEANWHILE, COOK THE BRUSSELS SPROUTS:
Boil a pot of salted water. Add the brussels sprouts and blanche for 3 minutes. Plunge them into cold water, then drain.

HEAT THE OLIVE OIL in a large nonstick skillet and fry the pancetta, garlic, and chili for 2 minutes, until golden. Add the sprouts and cook for 2 more minutes, constantly turning them. Season with salt and pepper. Keep warm.

FOR THE CELERY ROOT, heat the oil over medium heat in a large nonstick skillet, and cook the garlic until light brown. Add the pepper flakes, thyme, and celery root and mix thoroughly. Slowly add the stock, stirring. Simmer, adding more stock as it is absorbed, until the celeriac is soft, about 30 minutes. Mash coarsely and season with salt and pepper.

KERAMAS SNAPPER
WITH STIR-FRIED GINGER, CARROT, ASPARAGUS & BROCCOLINI

KERAMAS, SANUR, BALI, INDONESIA

An excellent but exposed right- and left-hand reef break on the east coast. This is often an uncrowded wave, and the locals are friendly, but surfing here means negotiating some nasty rips. When making this light and healthy lunch or dinner, use the freshest white fish you can find; red snapper is an awesome choice. This marinade combines two of my favorites: macadamia nuts and turmeric. A potent antioxidant pairing to boost your immune system.

SERVES 2 - TOTAL TIME: 30 MIN

2 snapper, tilapia, or sea bass fillets, boned and skinned

1 lime, halved

Vegetable oil, for cooking

1 lemon, sliced

Ingredients for the marinade:

3 macadamia nuts

4 shallots, minced

3 cloves garlic, crushed

1 Tbsp Laird Superfood Turmeric Creamer (or turmeric powder)

1 tsp ground coriander

Sea salt and black pepper

Ingredients for basting:

¼ cup soy sauce

1 Tbsp raw butter, melted

2 Tbsp vegetable oil

Ingredients for the stir fry:

1 Tbsp vegetable oil

1 Tbsp grated ginger

1 carrot, shredded

1 cup snow peas

1 cup asparagus tips

4 stalks broccolini

1 Tbsp soy sauce & 1 tsp rice vinegar

2 tsp mixed black & white sesame seeds

LIGHTLY SCORE THE FISH FILLETS in four places on one side and place in a baking dish, scored sides up; squeeze the lime juice over the fish.

PUT THE MARINADE ingredients in a food processor and blend until it forms a smooth paste. Spread the marinade over both sides of the fish, making sure it goes into the score marks. Cover and refrigerate for 1 hour.

COMBINE THE BASTING INGREDIENTS in a bowl. Heat a large nonstick ridged skillet over medium-high heat; evenly coat with vegetable oil. Add the fillets and cook about 3 minutes on each side, until cooked through. When the fish is almost done, baste both sides with prepared mixture. Keep warm.

FOR THE STIR-FRY heat a wok over high heat and add the vegetable oil. Add the ginger and cook for 30 seconds. Add the vegetables and stir-fry for 2 minutes, adding a splash of water if it seems dry. Remove from heat, then toss with soy and vinegar. Garnish with the sesame seeds.

SERVE FISH with a slice of lemon and the vegetables.

My surfing is all about the foil. This short, prone board
is the most efficient wave riding tool for big days.

YUMURI BBQ SEA BASS WITH ROASTED SWEET POTATOES & OKRA WITH SALSA VERDE

YUMURI, CUBA

While not famed as a surf destination, Cuba is the largest island in the Caribbean and has plenty of unexplored possibilities—although not that long ago local surfers were often arrested for trying to escape the island. This is a rivermouth break both right and left that only breaks in winter.

I love a whole fish! Suck the eyeballs, chew the head—this is how you should eat fish. It's served here with two authentic vegetable sides. Make plenty of the salsa verde; it's great with all types of meat and fish, hot or cold.

SERVES 1 - TOTAL TIME: 60 MIN

- **Ingredients for the fish:**
  1 whole sea bass (or similar)
      cleaned, scales intact
  Sea salt and black pepper
  1 sprig dill
  1 lemon, sliced

- **Ingredients for the vegetables:**
  1 large sweet potato,
      roughly cubed
  1 Tbsp olive oil
  6–8 whole okra
  1 clove garlic, minced
  1 Tbsp chopped parsley
  Juice of ½ lime
  Sea salt, black pepper

Preheat the oven to 425°F.

LIGHT A BBQ—whether gas or coal, get it good and hot. Wipe it down with oil to prevent the fish from sticking.

CUT FOUR SLASHES through the skin on each side of the fish (this will help it cook evenly). Coat the fish lightly in oil. Season with salt and pepper inside and out. Fill the inner cavity with fresh dill.

PREPARE THE SWEET POTATOES: Toss them in half of the oil and spread them at one end of a large rimmed roasting tray. Roast for 30 minutes. Toss the okra in the remaining oil, and add it to the other end of the pan. Cook for 15 minutes more, until both vegetables are nicely browned and becoming crispy. Toss the sweet potaoes with the garlic and parsley and squeeze the lime over. Season both vegetables with salt and pepper. Keep warm.

Ingredients for the salsa verde:

1 cup chopped fresh parsley

1 cup chopped fresh basil

½ cup chopped fresh mint

3 cloves garlic

4 oz capers, drained

4 oz anchovies, drained

2 Tbsp red wine vinegar

5 Tbsp olive oil

1 Tbsp Dijon mustard

Sea salt and black pepper

FOR THE SALSA VERDE, place all the ingredients in a food processor, and pulse-chop until roughly blended. Can be stored in an airtight container in the refrigerator for several days.

PUT THE FISH ON THE HOT GRILL so that the bars run horizontally down the length of the fish. This helps it not to stick. There will be smoke and fire as the oil drips through, but all this adds to the flavor. After about 8 minutes, carefully lift, ensuring the skin is not stuck to the grate, then flip onto the other side for another 8 minutes.

SERVE THE FISH WHOLE with lemon slices on top, salsa verde in a bowl on the side, and the roasted vegetables.

HONKY'S SQUASH KOFTAS IN MASALA CURRY SAUCE

HONKY'S, MALDIVES

These atolls are located right in the middle of the Indian Ocean and are fully exposed to the southern ocean swells. This North Male Atoll break is best in the summer months, it's a long, wrapping left-hander giving rides of over 100 yards long, buidling in height as it moves inside. The style of this Indian-influenced bowl is "street food," almost like tapas. The key ingredient, squash, is from the largest group of vegetables, and possibly the oldest cultivated crop, with archaelogical evidence from 10,000 years ago. Its seeds have been connected to antiparasitic strengths, protecting us from a variety of internal diseases.

SERVES 4 - TOTAL TIME: 60 MIN

- **Ingredients for the squash koftas:**
  1 ¼ lb butternut squash, finely grated
  ¼ cup gluten-free flour
  ¼ tsp garam marsala
  ⅓ tsp cayenne pepper
  1 green chili, minced & sea salt
  2 cups vegetable oil

- **Ingredients for the masala paste:**
  2 large tomatoes, chopped
  1 medium yellow onion, chopped
  1 green chili, chopped
  1 thumb ginger, chopped
  5 cloves garlic, chopped
  2 Tbsp cashews, broken

- **Ingredients for the sauce:**
  1 tsp ground cumin
  ¼ tsp cayenne pepper
  1 Tbsp Laird Superfood Turmeric
      Creamer (or 1 tsp turmeric powder)
  1 tsp ground coriander
  ¼ tsp garam marsala
  1 cup water & Sea salt
  ¼ cup chopped cilantro, for garnish

RINSE AND PEEL the squash. Divide it into easy-to-handle pieces, and grate it with a fine grater. Squeeze out the excess juice. Mix the rest of the kofta ingredients except the oil in a bowl with the squash. Scoop 3-inch round balls of the mixture.

HEAT THE OIL in a medium nonstick skillet and carefully fry the koftas, turning constantly, until golden brown all over. Drain on paper towels.

IN A BLENDER combine all the masala paste ingredients with a little water into a smooth paste.

FOR THE SAUCE, remove all but 2 tablespoons of the oil from the same skillet, and return it to the heat. Add the masala paste and cumin. Fry for 10 minutes, then add the other spices; stir in the water and season with salt. Simmer for another 10 minutes.

TO SERVE, pour the curry sauce into a small bowl and add the desired quantity of koftas. Garnish with fresh cilantro.

SUPERTUBOS PAELLA WITH CHICKEN, CHORIZO, CLAMS & MUSSELS

SUPERTUBOS, PENICHE, PORTUGAL

Regarded as the best wave in Portugal, this fast-barrelling tube has become a top stop on the pro world tour. Though not as notorious as Nazarre, it is definitely high performance in the winter months.

There's often debate about paella ingredients, which is why you are best customizing your own. I'm not a big fan of too much rice, but I love the combination of meat and crustaceans. This is a great, family-style experience, particularly if you can get your hands on a really big pan.

SERVES 6 - TOTAL TIME: 60 MIN

4 oz fresh chorizo,
    casing removed

1 small onion, thinly sliced

1 clove garlic, crushed

1 red bell pepper, trimmed,
    seeded, and cut into strips

½ cup garden peas

1 cup wild rice

Pinch of saffron

2 ½ cups vegetable broth

Sea salt and black pepper

1 Tbsp fresh lemon juice

½ lb mussels, shells cleaned

½ lb clams, shells cleaned

1 ½ cups cooked chicken

2 Tbsp chopped parsley,
    for garnish

2 green onions, sliced,
    for garnish

Preheat the oven to 350°F.

IN A 12-IN PAELLA PAN or ovenproof skillet over medium heat, cook the chorizo, breaking it up with a spoon, for 4 minutes, until browned. Lower the heat, add the onion and garlic, and cook for 8 minutes, until softened. Stir in the red pepper, peas, rice, saffron, and 2 cups of the vegetable broth. Season with salt and pepper. Cover and simmer over low heat until the rice is al dente and the liquid is absorbed, about 45 minutes. If the mixture begins to dry out, add a little more broth.

INTO A SEPARATE PAN, bring the remaining ½ cup broth and the lemon juice to a boil. Add the mussels and clams, cover, and cook, shaking the pan, until the shells open, approximately 3 minutes. Discard any closed shells, Pour the pan contents into the rice.

STIR THE COOKED CHICKEN into the rice. Cover and cook in the oven for about 5 minutes until paella is hot throughout. To serve, garnish with parsley and green onions.

TEMAE SPINY LOBSTER
WITH LEMON BUTTER & SAUTÉED SWEET POTATOES

TEMAE, MOOREA ISLAND, TAHITI

On just one of the 130 islands in this archipelago, the Temae break hugs the coastline shelf and comes very close to the beach, meaning the crowd gets a spectacular view of the right-hand barrel, similar to Backdoor on Hawaii's North Shore.

The Pacific spiny lobster has no claws, but a weighty tail. They are low in fat but packed with protein, making them perfect for athletes. This preparation is simple but highly effective given the rich, subtle flavor of this luxurious meat.

SERVES 2 - TOTAL TIME: 30 MIN

- **Ingredients for the lobster:**
  2 (5-oz) lobster tails
  4 Tbsp raw butter, cubed
  1 lemon, halved
- **Ingredients for the marinade:**
  1 Tbsp chopped parsley
  2 cloves garlic, crushed
  1 tsp Dijon mustard
  Sea salt and black pepper
  2 Tbsp olive oil
  2 Tbsp fresh lemon juice
- **Ingredients for the sweet potato:**
  2 Tbsp olive oil
  2 cups shredded sweet potato
  Sea salt and black pepper

TO PREPARE THE LOBSTER TAIL, use kitchen shears to cut through the shell top of the tail down to the base. Then do the same on the underside shell of the tail. Carefully use your fingers to loosen the meat and gently pull apart each half of the shell. Close the shell together while lifting up the meat, keeping attached at the base. The meat should now be presented on top of the shell.

PREHEAT THE OVEN to broil, with a rack 6 inches from the heating element.

FOR THE MARINADE, Combine the parsley, garlic, mustard, salt, pepper, oil, and lemon juice. Stir to combine.

PLACE THE LOBSTER tails side by side in a small roasting pan. Evenly spoon the marinade mixture over both lobster tails. Position raw butter cubes centrally on top.

BROIL THE LOBSTER tails for about 10 minutes; the meat should turn white and read 145°F on a cooking thermometer.

FOR THE SWEET POTATO, in a small nonstick skillet, heat the olive oil over medium-high heat. Add the sweet potato and sauté for a couple of minutes until it begins to brown. Season with salt and pepper to taste.

SERVE the lobster tails on top of the nest of sweet potato, together with an extra lemon half.

TRIGG POINT SAUTEED TURKEY MEATBALLS

WITH TOMATO & ONION SAUCE ON SPAGHETTI SQUASH

TRIGG POINT, PERTH, AUSTRALIA

Perth's most reliable but overcrowded right-hander, where the wave peels perfectly over a sand-covered reef. Turkey, with fewer calories and less fat than the same portion of beef, this is a great meatball alternative, and aids in the production of niacin and serotonin, brain chemicals that help to balance your mood.

SERVES 4 - TOTAL TIME: 60 MIN

Ingredients for the sauce:

1 Tbsp olive oil

1 cup chopped yellow onion

2 cloves garlic, crushed

1 (28-oz) can crushed
  tomatoes

1 Tbsp chopped parsley

4 bay leaves

Sea salt and black pepper

Ingredients for the squash:

1 medium spaghetti squash

1 Tbsp olive oil

Ingredients for the meatballs:

1 lb ground turkey

3 cloves garlic, minced

¼ cup finely chopped
  yellow onion

¼ cup chopped parsley

½ tsp dried oregano

1 egg, beaten

½ cup gluten-free flour

Sea salt and black pepper

1 Tbsp olive oil

Preheat the oven to 400°F.

FOR THE SAUCE, heat the oil in a nonstick skillet over medium-high heat. Add the onion and garlic and sauté until soft and translucent, about 3 minutes. Add the tomatoes, parsley, and bay leaves. Season with salt and pepper. Simmer, covered, on low for 1 hour, until thick.

SLICE THE SQUASH in half lengthwise and carefully scoop out the seeds with a spoon. Place the two halves cut sides down in a roasting pan. Cook for 30 to 45 minutes, depending on size of squash, until tender. Use a fork to separate the flesh into spaghetti-like strands. Transfer the squash into a bowl and toss with a little oil.

COMBINE AND MIX all of the meatball ingredients except the olive oil in a bowl. Shape 12 meatballs of approximately 2 inches in diameter.

HEAT THE OIL in a nonstick skillet over medium-high heat. Add as many meatballs as the pan allows, without crowding them. Cook for about 6 minutes, until cooked through and nicely browned. Repeat with the remaining meatballs.

ASSEMBLE IN INDIVIDUAL BOWLS. Serve two large serving spoonfuls of squash into each bowl, place three meatballs in the middle, and pour tomato sauce evenly over the top.

My dog Kawa regularly watches my sessions from the boat,
but needs discipling from afar.

LITTLE DuME GRILLED T-BONE STEAK

& ROASTED RED POTATOES, RADISHES WITH FENNEL & LEMON BUTTER SAUCE

LITTLE DuME, PARADISE COVE, MALIBU, USA

My wave during the summer months, Little Dume delivers a flawless point break from the right, but it's pretty much locals only, because it is not easy to access. This beautiful porterhouse steak is cut from the short loin. Cooking with the bone in has the advantage of the meat cooking evenly and without shrinking, This is without a doubt my favorite steak.

SERVES 4 - TOTAL TIME: 30 MIN

Ingredients for vegetables:

1 lb small red potatoes

2 Tbsp olive oil

Sea salt and black pepper

1 lb radishes, trimmed and halved

1 fennel bulb, cut lengthwise
   into eighths

¼ cup raw butter

Juice of ½ lemon

½ tsp Dijon mustard

½ tsp maple syrup

1 tsp chopped fresh mint, garnish

Ingredients for the steaks:

4 (28-oz) T-bone steaks, bone in

Sea salt and black pepper

2 Tbsp olive oil

Preheat the oven to 450°F.

CUT THE POTATOES into quarters and toss with 1 tablespoon of the olive oil in a large bowl. Season with salt and pepper. Spread the potatoes on a rimmed baking tray and roast for 10 minutes. Toss the radishes and fennel with the remaining tablespoon of the olive oil and season with salt and pepper. Add the radishes and fennel to the tray and roast for 15 minutes.

MEANWHILE, MELT THE BUTTER in a small saucepan over medium heat, about 4 minutes. Remove from the stove and whisk in the lemon juice, mustard, and maple syrup. When the vegetables are ready, mix them with the butter sauce and garnish with mint. Keep warm.

THE BEST WAY to cook a T-bone steak is over high, direct heat, then move to indirect heat to finish cooking. Season the steaks generously with salt and pepper. Heat 1 tablepoon of the olive oil in a nonstick, ridged grill pan over high heat. When it begins to smoke, add two steaks and cook for 4 minutes on each side, until the grill marks are all over. Repeat with the remaining steaks. Transfer to the oven and roast until a cooking thermometer reads 120°F for medium-rare, 6 to 8 minutes. Let them rest for 10 minutes before serving.

YOU CAN CUT THE MEAT from the bone and carve across the grain, or serve it on the bone. Serve with roasted vegetables.

KAMALA GRILLED SALMON WITH CUCUMBER & RED ONION SALSA

WITH WILD RICE & SWEET CHILI DIPPING SAUCE

KAMALA, PHUKET, THAILAND

The northerly beach of Kamala, on the country's largest island is a popular surf destination, and has a beach break and a point break, both working best during the summer months of May to October. Famously featured in James Bond's *The Man with the Golden Gun*, this coastline is iconic. Cooking the rice will slow you down, but this simple marinade results in a sweet, crunchy sear that is hard to beat. The cilantro is the surprise ingredient here, loaded with antioxidants, vitamin A, vitamin C, and minerals like phosphorus, which help prevent vision disorders and muscular degeneration.

SERVES 4 - TOTAL TIME: 45 MIN

4 wild-caught salmon steaks

1 red chili pepper, minced

2 cloves garlic, crushed

¼ cup chopped cilantro

1 Tbsp fish sauce

1 Tbsp toasted sesame oil

2 Tbsp local honey

Sea salt and black pepper

¼ cucumber, diced

½ red onion, diced

* **Ingredients for the dipping sauce:**

1 cup rice wine vinegar

½ cup Laird Superfood coconut sugar

¼ cup finely chopped cilantro

Pinch of red pepper flakes

* **2 cups cooked forbidden rice**

Preheat a grill pan.

PUT THE SALMON steaks in a low bowl and marinate with the chili, garlic, cilantro, fish sauce, sesame oil, and honey. Season with salt and pepper. Refrigerate for at least 20 minutes or overnight.

TOSS the cucumber and onion together.

FOR THE DIPPING SAUCE, put the vinegar and sugar in a small pan over medium-high heat and bring to a boil. Cool, then add the cilantro and red pepper flakes. Place in small bowls for dipping.

GRILL the salmon until crisp around the edges, about 3 minutes each side; it should be firm to the touch.

SERVE with the cucumber and onion salsa on the top and the rice and dipping sauce on the side.

BANYANS HALIBUT WITH MACADAMIA NUT CRUST & RICED BROCCOLI WITH TURMERIC COCONUT SAUCE

BANYANS, BIG ISLAND, HAWAII, USA

The one principal Hawaiian island I have never lived on. This exposed reef break is popular with the locals and produces year-round waves. Be careful of the urchins on the rocky sea floor. This dish features many of my favorite things in one place! The sauce I have created here using my Turmeric Superfood Creamer is the magic that binds it together. Most interesting about the anti-inflammatory turmeric is that where it is consumed in the highest quantities, common cancer types are less prevalent.

SERVES 4 - TOTAL TIME: 45 MIN

Ingredients for the turmeric-coconut sauce:

1 Tbsp coconut oil
½ yellow onion, chopped
1 clove garlic, minced
1 thumb ginger, peeled and minced
½ cup vegetable broth
2 Tbsp Laird Superfood Turmeric Creamer (or 1 tsp ground tumeric)
¼ tsp ground cinnamon
Pinch of sea salt
¾ cup coconut milk
Juice of ½ lemon

Ingredients for the fish:

2 slices gluten-free bread
½ cup roasted macadamia nuts
1 egg
4 (6-oz) Pacific halibut steaks

Preheat the oven to 350°F.

PREPARE THE SAUCE. Heat the coconut oil in a medium pan over medium heat. Add the onion and cook for 5 minutes, until translucent. Add the garlic and ginger; cook, stirring, for 1 minute. Add the broth, turmeric, cinnamon, and salt. Simmer for 10 minutes. Let cool.

PLACE THE COCONUT milk and lemon juice in a blender and add the turmeric mixture; blend until smooth. Return to a clean pan and keep warm.

TO MAKE THE NUT CRUST, toast the bread and blitz in a food processor until you have coarse breadcrumbs. Add the macadamia nuts and pulse again until texture is consistent. Tip onto a plate.

BEAT THE EGG in a shallow bowl. Season the fish steaks with salt and pepper on both sides. Dredge them in the egg wash, then coat them in the nut mixture.

HEAT THE COCONUT OIL in a nonstick, ovenproof skillet over medium-high heat. When oil is boiling, add the fish and fry about 2 minutes per side, until golden. Transfer to oven and cook 5 minutes, or until cooked.

Sea salt and black pepper

¼ cup coconut oil

Chives, for garnish

1 head riced broccoli or riced
   cauliflower

SERVE THE FISH on top of a bed of riced broccoli or riced cauliflower. Pour the turmeric sauce over the top. Garnish with chives.

CUT THE FLORETS off the broccoli head into the bowl of a food processor. Pulse into pieces the size of grains of rice. In a frying pan, heat the coconut oil over medium heat, add the broccoli 'rice' and lightly cook for 4–6 minutes, or until softened. Season with salt and pepper and serve.

GREEN BOWL CHICKEN CURRY
WITH GREEN BEANS, BELL PEPPERS & BASIL

GREEN BOWL, BALI, INDONESIA

I loved it here: the Island of the Gods. This break is secluded—you have to trek down many cliffside steps to access it—but it's rewardingly quiet and uncrowded when you get there. Whether it be green or red, a simple bowl of aromatic and fresh curry is easily customized to fit your taste and the local ingredients available. Good quantities of the legendary holy basil are recommended.

SERVES 4 - TOTAL TIME: 30 MIN

Ingredients for the green curry paste:

2 tsp ground cumin

2 tsp ground coriander

2 green chilis, seeded and minced

1 shallot, chopped

1 thumb ginger, peeled & chopped

2 cloves garlic

Grated zest of 1 lime

1 stalk lemongrass, white root
  end only, outer leaves peeled,
  roughly chopped

¼ cup chopped cilantro

1 tsp fish sauce

Ingredients for the chicken curry:

2 large boneless skinless chicken breasts

Pinch of sea salt

1 Tbsp coconut oil

1 shallot, sliced thin

1 (14-oz) can coconut milk, shaken

1 red bell pepper, trimmed,
  seeded, cut into strips

½ lb green beans, trimmed

¼ cup whole basil leaves

¼ cup whole cilantro leaves

4 lime wedges, for serving

MAKE THE GREEN CURRY PASTE by combining all the ingredients in a food processor. Blend until smooth, scraping down the sides with a rubber spatula. This makes double the quantity required, but you can freeze the remainder.

SEASON THE CHICKEN breasts with salt. Cut across the grain into thin strips. Set a wok or large skillet over high heat and add the coconut oil. When hot, add the chicken and sear for 5 minutes. Transfer to a plate.

LOWER THE HEAT to medium-high. Add the shallot to the wok and cook for 1 minute; add 2 generous spoonfuls of the curry paste. Cook for 1 minute. Add the coconut milk and stir constantly, scraping the edges of the pan.

ADD the cooked chicken strips, bell pepper, and beans. Reduce the heat to low and cook for 20 minutes. Remove from heat and stir in the fresh basil and cilantro. Serve with lime wedges.

CHICAMA BEEF STIR-FRY WITH ONION, BELL PEPPERS, GARLIC & HAND-MADE OVEN FRIES

CHICAMA, PERU

Halfway between Lima and the Ecuadorian border, Chicama is undoubtedly the longest wave in the world. I recently visited with friends, and we were stand-up foiling uninterrupted for two and a half miles at a time! Waving down a zodiac, and doing it again, and again, and again. In four days we rode in excess of 100 miles.

This is traditional Peruvian cooking that is easy to make and popular with both adults and kids. It breaks the rules of rice-and-stir-fry with potato fries, which is exactly why I love it, particularly after eight hours a day on the water.

SERVES 4 - TOTAL TIME: 30 MIN

1 cup wild rice

8 large red potatoes

1 cup vegetable oil

48 oz rib-eye steak

Sea salt and black pepper

2 cloves garlic, crushed

1 red onion, thinly sliced

1 red bell pepper, trimmed,
    seeded, cut into strips

1 green bell pepper, trimmed,
    seeded, cut into strips

1 Tbsp red wine vinegar

1 Tbsp soy sauce

½ cup vegetable broth

2 Tbsp chopped parsley,
    for garnish

PREPARE THE RICE according to the instructions on the package. This takes about 45 minutes.

MEANWHILE, PEEL THE POTATOES and trim each so it's one block, then cut into equal-size fries. Place a medium skillet over high heat. Add ½ cup of the oil and, when it's hot, fry the fries, turning regularly, until golden, about 15 minutes. Set aside on paper towel to drain. Dispose of all but ¼ cup of oil.

CUT THE STEAK into long strips of about ¼-inch thickness and 2 inches in length. Season with salt, pepper, and garlic.

RETURN THE SKILLET to medium heat. Once the oil is very hot, add the steak and stir constantly to sear all sides. After a couple of minutes, add the onion and cook until softened. Add the bell peppers, vinegar, and soy. Pour in the broth and simmer until the peppers are tender.

COMBINE the beef mixture with the cooked rice and serve with the fries; garnish with parsley.

LA CHAPELLE CHICKEN CASSOULET WITH OLIVE, SAUSAGE, PARMA, ROSEMARY, GARLIC, CANNELLINI BEANS & FENNEL

LA CHAPELLE, BRITTANY, FRANCE

Another regional throwback on the cold Atlantic ocean. A rugged, rocky reef break that comes alive in the foggy depths of winter. Uncrowded, even when there are waves, this largely untouched coast produces some regular but varied conditions, albeit accompanied by cold temperatures and brutal winds.

This is a hearty, seasonal, and magnificent French casserole. Fennel gets the shout-out here, with a long list of health benefits, most interestingly as an aid to digestion. It's equally great as a drink; fennel tea's calming effect soothes your system.

SERVES 4 - TOTAL TIME: 120 MIN

2 garlic bulbs, halved

2 fennel bulbs, quartered

1 ¼ cups olive oil

4 large chicken quarters, skin on (best to buy in pre-cut quarters, breast with leg)

4 tsp black olive spread

4 spicy sausages

½ Tbsp whole black peppercorns

Sea salt

4 rosemary sprigs

2 lemons, juiced and halved

4 cups chicken broth

2 (15-oz) cans cannellini beans, drained

4 oz Parma ham

Preheat the oven to 400°F

PLACE THE GARLIC AND FENNEL in a large deep, roasting tray, coat in ¼ cup of olive oil, and roast for 25 minutes.

LOOSEN THE SKIN OF THE CHICKEN QUARTERS with your fingers to create a pocket, then tuck 1 teaspoon of the olive spread underneath each. Heat up 3 tablespoons of the olive oil in a large nonstick skillet. Add the chicken, skin side down, and cook for 4 minutes, until really golden, then turn over and fry the other side for 1 minute. Remove to a plate. In the same pan, lower the heat, add the sausages, and brown them all over.

WHEN the fennel and garlic are ready, add the chicken, sausage, peppercorns, salt, rosemary, lemon juice, and the squeezed lemon halves. Pour the remaining olive oil over. Roast for 45 minutes.

REMOVE from the oven and add the broth and beans. Return to the oven and bake for 15 minutes. Place the Parma ham slices on top and bake for another 15 minutes.

GRAND HAVEN BISON CHILI WITH HOMEMADE CORN TORTILLA CHIPS

GRAND HAVEN, LAKE MICHIGAN, USA

When a lake is 22,300 square miles in size, the third largest in the USA, there are going to be waves. Grand Haven is surf central in Michigan, and this break happens right off the pier with a left and a right. Often the waves are a little messy and the rip can have serious consequences. After a cold session here, a bowl of chili might be the answer. This uses local midwest bison, which is almost fat free and contains more than 40 percent more protein than beef. Find an organic source where these animals have spent their lives on grass and avoided questionable drugs and hormones.

SERVES 4 - TOTAL TIME: 90 MIN

4 corn tortillas

Sea salt and black pepper

2 Tbsp olive oil

2 medium onions, finely chopped

2 cloves garlic, crushed

1 Tbsp paprika

1 tsp red pepper flakes

1 tsp ground cumin

1 tsp ground coriander

1 lb ground organic bison

¼ lb mushrooms, chopped

1 (28-oz) can chopped tomatoes

1 cup beef broth

3 Tbsp tomato paste

1 Tbsp dried oregano

2 tsp dried basil

2 tsp dried savory

½ tsp dried thyme

2 bay leaves

2 Tbsp masa harina

2 green onions, chopped, for garnish

1 Tbsp chopped fresh cilantro, for garnish

Preheat the oven to 350°F.

CUT THE TORTILLAS into triangles. Spread them out on a large baking tray. Bake for about 6 minutes, then use tongs to turn them over. Season with some sea salt and bake for another 10 minutes, until crisp and golden. Set aside to cool.

IN A LARGE SAUCEPAN, heat the oil over medium heat. Add the onions, garlic, paprika, red pepper flakes, cumin, and coriander and sauté for 4 minutes. Add the bison, increase the heat to high, and thoroughly brown the meat for 10 minutes, breaking the meat up as you go. Stir in the mushrooms, tomatoes, broth, tomato paste, and herbs. Bring to a boil, then reduce the heat and simmer briskly for about 1 ½ hours, stirring occasionally.

THE CHILI SHOULD BE THICK but still slightly liquid at this point. Stir in the masa harina and simmer for 15 minutes. Discard the bay leaves and serve in bowls with homemade tortilla chips. Garnish with green onions and cilantro.

BONDI GLUTEN-FREE BREADED TILAPIA WITH ZESTY ARUGULA, RADISH & CUCUMBER SALAD

BONDI, SYDNEY, AUSTRALIA

Hawaiian Duke Kahanamoku brought surfing to Sydney in about 1915. Bondi is just east of the city and home to Bondi Rescue, the world-famous lifeguards who rescue and protect the enormous crowds here daily. There is an exposed beach break that is reliable all year-round, where you'll find the surfers at the south end and boogie boarders and bodysurfers at the north end.

Baking your fish is a great option, and healthier than frying. I love to try variations on the breadcrumb mixture. This one recommends Parmesan, the healthiest and longest-aged of all cheeses, packed with protein, calcium, and vitamin A. It should be regarded as a superfood.

SERVES 2 - TOTAL TIME: 30 MIN

Ingredients for the fish:

½ cup olive oil, additional for pan

2 tilapia fillets

1 Tbsp lemon juice

Sea salt and black pepper

¾ cup grated Parmesan cheese (optional)

¾ cup gluten-free breadcrumbs

1 tsp garlic powder

1 tsp paprika

½ tsp red pepper flakes

½ tsp dried parsley

1 lemon, sliced

Ingredients for the salad:

4 cups arugula (packed)

½ cup thinly sliced radishes

1 cup thinly sliced cucumber

2 Tbsp olive oil

2 Tbsp white wine vinegar

Grated zest of ½ lemon

Preheat oven to 400°F.

LINE A RIMMED BAKING TRAY with aluminum foil and lightly grease with olive oil.

IN A SHALLOW BOWL, combine the tilapia, olive oil, lemon juice, salt, and pepper. Marinate for 30 minutes.

IN A SEPARATE SHALLOW BOWL, mix together the Parmesan, breadcrumbs, garlic powder, paprika, red pepper flakes, and parsley. Press each tilapia fillet into the mixture, covering both sides thoroughly. Place the fillets on the prepared baking tray. Bake for 20 minutes, until golden and cooked through.

FOR THE SALAD, combine the arugula and vegetables in a mixing bowl and drizzle the olive oil and vinegar over. Zest the lemon over the top.

SERVE EACH FISH fillet with a slice of lemon.

A magical first-light paddle down in Cabo San Lucas, Mexico.

FOURTH SESSION

KAHALU'U CHILLED CHOCOLATE AVOCADO MOUSSE CAKE

KAHALU'U, BIG ISLAND, HAWAII, USA

One of the best spots on the Kona coast for every level of skill, Kahalu'u is an amazing reef that, though shallow and dangerous for surfing, is ideal for stand-up paddling and snorkeling adventures, with an abundance of colorful fish, manta rays, and turtles. No cooking required, and with a unsuspected secret ingredient: avocado. This ingredient actually contains more potassium than a banana. A healthy intake of potassium has been linked to reduced blood presssure, which helps us avoid heart attack and strokes.

SERVES 8 - TOTAL TIME: 135 MIN

🏴 **Ingredients for the base:**

2 Tbsp coconut oil,
   plus more for the pan
2 cups pecans
¼ cup Laird Superfood Cacao Creamer (or cacao powder)
¼ cup pure maple syrup
1 tsp vanilla extract
½ tsp sea salt

🏴 **Ingredients for the mousse:**

2 large mashed avocados
⅓ cup almond milk
⅔ cup pure maple syrup
1 Tbsp smooth cashew butter
1 Tbsp arrowroot powder
¼ tsp sea salt
1 tsp vanilla extract
¼ cup Laird Superfood Cacao Creamer (or cacao powder)
1 cup organic chocolate chips

FOR THE BASE, lightly oil a 10-in springform pan. **PULSE THE PECANS** in a food processor until they resemble coarse breadcrumbs. Add the remaining ingredients and quickly pulse to combine. Spoon the mixture into the pan and distribute evenly, pressing down firmly with a spatula. Place in the freezer to set.

FOR THE MOUSSE, put all the ingredients except the chocolate chips in the food processor. Blend until smooth. Melt the chocolate chips in a microwave or in a bowl over some boiling water. Add melted chocolate to the mousse mixture and blend until smooth.

REMOVE THE BASE from the freezer and spoon on the mousse. Spread and smooth out as much as possible with a rubber spatula. Return to the freezer for 2 hours to firm up.

HAIKU BANANA BREAD WITH GRILLED PINEAPPLE
YOGURT & MINT

HAIKU, MAUI, HAWAII

Not technically a break, but my old home, literally, and the home of my number one: Pe'ahi or Jaws. My friends and I started windsurfing on this break—an iconic monster—from close-by Ho'okipa Beach in the 1980s, later to conquer it on tow-in boards. The submerged volcanic topography produces the very largest waves on the planet. Indigenous to the cliffs above this location are acres of pineapple fields. Historically, Hawaii was the largest producer in the world. Pineapples contain bromelain, an enzyme said to stimulate digestion, improve heart health, and protect against some cancers.

SERVES 8 - TOTAL TIME: 50 MIN

½ cup raw butter, softened,
  plus more for the pan

2 cups gluten-free flour

1 tsp baking soda

1 tsp baking powder

Pinch of salt

½ cup coconut sugar

2 eggs

2 Tbsp coconut milk

½ tsp vanilla extract

1 ½ cups mashed ripe bananas

Fresh pineapple slices

Plain yogurt

2 mint leaves, chiffonaded,
  for garnish

Preheat the oven to 350°F.

Lightly grease a 9-in-x-5-in loaf pan.

IN A LARGE MIXING BOWL, combine the flour, baking soda, baking powder, and salt.

IN ANOTHER BOWL, whisk the butter and coconut sugar. Then stir in the eggs, coconut milk, vanilla, and mashed bananas until completely mixed. Stir the banana mixture into the flour mixture and pour into the loaf pan.

BAKE for about 50 minutes, until a knife inserted into the loaf comes out clean.

Let the bread cool on a rack.

THE PINEAPPLE SLICES can be grilled or fried in a skillet with a little raw butter. Either way, you want to see the fruit begin to color and caramelize.

TO SERVE, TOP SLICES of banana bread with the pineapple and some plain yogurt. Garnish with mint.

HIGGINS MIXED-BERRY COBBLER

HIGGINS, MAINE, USA

A modest beach break that can reach a decent height in the fall with tropical storms coming up from the south. In the summer, the beach is actually closed to surfers, but in the freezing depths of winter, there is a resilient community of riders having a ball out there.

This recipe is super easy and perfect for using up half-empty trays of berries. You can also top this off with the porridge mix featured earlier in the book (page 16). A spoonful of plain yogurt is also a great addition to this traditional crumble dessert.

SERVES 4 - TOTAL TIME: 40 MIN

Ingredients for the fruit:

1 cup blueberries

1 cup raspberries

1 cup blackberries

1 cup quartered strawberries

3 Tbsp maple syrup

1 tsp ground cinnamon

1 tsp tapioca flour

Ingredients for the crust:

3 Tbsp coconut oil, melted, plus more for ramekins

⅓ cup almond flour

⅓ cup tapioca flour

½ cup rolled oats

1 ½ tsp baking powder

3 Tbsp almond milk

1 tsp vanilla extract

2 Tbsp Laird Superfood coconut sugar

1 tsp ground cinnamon

Preheat the oven to 350°F. Grease four ramekins with a little coconut oil.

IN A MIXING BOWL combine the blueberries, raspberries, blackberries, strawberries, maple syrup, cinnamon, and tapioca flour. Spoon the mixture evenly into the prepared ramekins.

IN A BOWL, COMBINE THE ALMOND FLOUR, tapioca flour, oats, baking powder, coconut oil, almond milk, vanilla, and 1 tablespoon of the coconut sugar. Mix thoroughly until smooth, and spread evenly on the top of each berry dish.

SPRINKLE THE REST of the coconut sugar and a pinch of cinnamon over the crust of each dessert. Bake for 25 minutes and serve immediately.

SHIPWRECKS BANANA ROLLED IN GRANOLA FRIED IN HONEY & CINNAMON

SHIPWRECKS, BAJA PENINSULA, MEXICO

Close to Cabo San Lucas, this reef and point break has some great long and fast surf, mainly in the summer months. Access is by a very rough road for about an hour and a half, but that doesn't keep the crowds away, and most people seem to make camp. This recipe should be illegal! But as a family we have this perfected. Whenever possible we use the smaller, naturally ripened apple bananas. They have the most intense flavor and are a better size for pan frying.

SERVES 4 - TOTAL TIME: 10 MIN

2 cups homemade granola
   (page 34)
8 apple bananas (if available,
   or 4 regular bananas)
2 Tbsp raw butter
½ cup local honey
1 tsp ground cinnamon

POUR THE GRANOLA ONTO a large plate. Peel the bananas and roll them in the granola, pushing the mixture into the flesh, completely encasing the fruit.

PLACE A LARGE NONSTICK skillet over medium-high heat. Add the raw butter, honey, and cinnamon and stir to combine. When hot, cook the bananas in two batches, carefully frying them in the mixture, turning frequently for only a couple of minutes, until caramelized and golden. Serve hot.

BALANCING YOUR DIET

In this section we share some simple nutritional facts and opinions that we hope might help you balance your weekly menu choices. Once again, my philosophy is simple, "Everything in moderation, including moderation." You should not worry about every meal, every day—but try and keep a healthy balance across the week. For example, if you eat meat and fish, then aim to eat a couple of fish recipes per week, perhaps two vegetarian plates, a poultry dish and a red meat meal.

We will also summarize the science of fueling up, the health benefits, and some of the precautions necessary with certain ingredient components. All of which play significant roles in the complex symphony of correctly fueling our systems. And perhaps most important of all, taking your water intake seriously. The body needs to be well hydrated for you to digest correctly, to know when you are hungry and to ensure the overall performance of all your organs.

The third criteria to maintaining this balanced approach is trying to use high quality, natural ingredients, the best that you can find or afford. We encourage you to try to connect with your local suppliers and farms, where there are organic products that will be probably be the healthiest and tastiest possible. Remember: When it comes to fruit and vegetables, looks can be deceiving. Some of the most perfect supermarket fruit and vegetable specimens can be watery and tasteless, whereas the odd looking, homegrown equivalent that has been left to nature will usually deliver better flavor. With the amount of chemicals, processes, and enhancements that mass food producers use for increasing profits, lengthening shelf life and bolstering volume, it is important to remember almost every step between the farm to the table means compromise.

The final, most important step, is to celebrate your creativity and the provenance of your cooking! The eclectic recipes we've selected in this book have been complied to offer balance to your menu, and to be straightforward in preparation and hopefully within the grasp of most. We have tried to avoid lengthy, technical directions and have written our recipes in a concise style that should deliver the dish, while being open to some interpretation. Despite the mouthwatering photography that you can almost taste, we are not chasing perfection in this book. The recipes are simply a selection of healthy and delicious options that deliver the diversity and balance that keep me interested in my food and fueled up for maximum performance.

Previous pages: Just another life training method to keep your hand-eye coordination as sharp as possible!
Opposite page: Low hanging fruit! An avocado half the size a human head, simply stunning.

DEALING WITH DAIRY

If you are on a strict Paleo or vegan diet, you will be avoiding dairy completely. Dairy can also be very challenging on some people's immune system when there is an inability to breakdown an enzyme called lactase, which breaks down the natural sugars found in dairy. In moderation, however, there are key nutrients that help keep us strong and healthy: The protein contained in dairy is crucial for cell growth and repair; calcium is widely recognized for strong bones and healthy teeth particularly in developing children; riboflavin contributes to healthy skin and assists in the digestion of carbohydrates; iodine plays a part in metabolism regulation, which ensures the healthy function of the thyroid gland.

In theory, dairy should only be 15 percent of a balanced diet. In this book, we use small amounts of dairy throughout, which are often replaceable with a selection of substitute products. The organic argument also exists here. When you can ensure that cows have been grazing on chemical-free grass, and that they have not been pumped with antibiotics, they will have lived a longer, healthier life—with benefits to you as the consumer of their dairy.

We use raw butter and sometimes raw milk in our cooking, and despite being unpasteurized they are both completely safe. It is the manipulation of many dairy products that has been implicated in allergies and even heart disease. That said, most alternatives to dairy milk are fortified with the calcium and vitamins that emulate the benefits of dairy milk. I favor organic soy, almond or hemp milk, all of which are high in protein and low in saturated fats.

> **"I ALSO LOVE COCONUT MILK BECAUSE IT CONTAINS A BENEFICIAL FAT CALLED LAURIC ACID, WHICH IS A MEDIUM-CHAIN FATTY ACID THAT IS EASILY ABSORBED INTO THE BODY FOR ENERGY."**

It is best to choose the unsweetened variants. These are primarily saturated fats, but they are proven not to raise cholesterol or cause heart disease, in fact they do the opposite. As an alternative source of calcium, there are many plant based foods that offer huge amounts of the mineral plus a wealth of other health benefits. For example, kale offers very absorbable calcium and is also loaded with flavonoids and a very potent antioxidant.

Opposite page: The Okinawa purple sweet potato farmed locally at Kolo Kai Organic farm on Kauai.

HEALTHY FRUITS & VEGETABLES

Fruits and vegetables are central to a well-balanced diet. As you will read throughout the recipes in this book, the abundance of vitamins and minerals in fruits and vegetables boast medicinal properties and incredible powers for wellness.

We are very fortunate to have amazing local farm produce both in Kauai and on the mainland in California. Whenever possible, try to eat what is grown in your approximate area, or better yet, eat organic. Having knowledge about the health benefits and cautions associated with produce farming is valuable.

Eating conventionally grown fruits and vegetables is certainly better than not eating any at all, but we have to try to stay conscious of the toxic load some methods of growing put on our bodies. Produce can be full of pesticides, GMOs, and synthetic fertilizers, and with an accumulation in our system, these can create a myriad of issues. People will always criticize organic food because it's more expensive, which it is, but surely our bodies are worth looking after, and when you can eat the freshest food that's been grown naturally, you will be rewarded with better health.

> **"WHEN IT COMES TO HOW MUCH ONE SHOULD BE EATING DAILY, AIM HIGH. YOU SHOULD TRY TO GET SEVEN OR EIGHT SERVINGS THROUGHOUT THE DAY. BE EXPERIMENTAL. TRY TO CHOOSE THE MOST DIVERSE COLOR RANGE POSSIBLE TO REAP THE BENEFITS OF DIFFERENT NUTRIENTS AND THEIR POWERS ON OFFER."**

If you look around the world, the countries where people grow their own food seem to live the longest. Of course, when living in a climate with ground frosts and so on, you have to purchase certain imported produce. But it is extremely satisfying to try growing some of your own. I get the biggest kick out of our avocado orchard in Hawaii, where growing a selection of varieties means that we can harvest most of the year.

Opposite page: Support your locals farmer's market for the healthiest organic seasonal fruit and vegetables.

GOOD FAT

Despite the preconceptions that fats are bad, they are actually quite the opposite. Dietary fats are essential to provide us energy. Fats are also the way we store excess food energy. These reserves can then be called upon when food is in short supply. Once again, the key is moderation, otherwise we can gain weight by storing too much.

Fat provides vital protection to your internal organs, while also keeping your body warm. Additionally, the consumption of fats helps the body absorb certain nutrients and produce important hormones. A good example is using an oil-based salad dressing, this ensures that the vegetable's vitamins are absorbed effectively.

The healthiest type of fat is unsaturated, where the fatty acid is either monounsaturated or polyunsaturated. These can be found in most liquid vegetable oils, as well as nuts, legumes, avocados, and oily fish. On the other hand, saturated fats are animal-based, such as butter and meat fat. These fats raise cholesterol levels, and we need to be cautious when consuming them. The least-healthy type of fats are trans fats, which are industrially produced and mainly associated with processed snacks and fast food.

While all fats should be consumed in moderation, the general guide for an average man would be 90 grams a day, with less than 30 grams coming from saturates. For an average woman, approximately 70 grams per day is recommended, with less than 20 grams from saturated fat. Oils are also fat, and they are one of the healthiest ways to get fat into your system. We keep a selection of different types of oils, starting with extra virgin olive oil, which is loaded with omega-9 and reserved for the best salad dressings. For a less expensive frying oil, we use sunflower oil, which is rich in omega-6 and vitamin E. But my favorite, and the king of healthy fat, is avocado oil, super concentrated in monounsaturated fats, omega-9 and vitamin E.

> ❝ THE IMPORTANT THING ABOUT MAKING HEALTHY FAT WORK FOR YOU IS TO NOT CONSUME IT WITH SUGARS OR CARBOHYDRATES. FATS PAIRED WITH PROTEIN ARE GOOD, BUT EATING EVEN HEALTHY FAT WITH SUGAR OR CARBS CAN HAVE THE OPPOSITE RESULT YOU ARE LOOKING FOR. ❞

Opposite page: Some stunning Okinawa sweet potatoes grown by my friends at Kolo Kai organic farm on Kauai.

PROTEIN POWER

Talking protein gets very technical very quickly, but essentially our cells need these large molecules to function properly. The structure and function of the human body relies on proteins to regulate our cells, tissues, and organs. Our muscles, bones, and skin contain large amounts of protein, including enzymes, hormones, and antibodies. Hemoglobin, the carrier of oxygen in the blood stream, is a protein.

Proteins are made up of amino acids, and amino acids are the building blocks of our bodies. There are around twenty amino acids, which can be arranged in millions of different ways to create millions of different proteins, all of which have a specific function in the body. There are nine essential amino acids that the human body does not produce, so these are required in our diet. Foods that contain these nine essential acids in roughly equal proportions are called complete proteins. Complete proteins mainly come from animal sources, such as milk, meat, and eggs. Then there are incomplete proteins, such as beans, nuts, seeds, lentils, cereals, quinoa, oats, peas, bread, flour, and corn. It is necessary to combine these with other proteins in order to get the required volume of amino acids.

> "THERE CONTINUES TO BE A DEBATE ABOUT THE CORRECT AMOUNT OF PROTEIN WE SHOULD CONSUME. AGE, GENDER, AND ACTIVITY LEVEL ALL PLAY A ROLE IN DETERMINING OUR OPTIMAL INTAKE. AS A GENERAL GUIDE, APPROXIMATELY ONE-SIXTH OF OUR DAILY PLATE SHOULD BE MADE UP OF PROTEIN."

This amounts to about 45 grams a day for adult women and 55 grams for adult men. For those of us who are super active, these amounts can be nearly double, but as a family, we have cut back in favor of healthy fats. Once again, the organic preference applies. For me, there is no point in eating poor-quality meat, so I try to stick to locally farmed animals that have been well-fed and allowed to roam free. I actually opt for gamey meats, because I know they are less likely to have been tampered with.

For vegetarians and vegans, the protein requirement takes a bit more effort. The highest-protein performers include: quinoa, buckwheat, soy, mycoprotein, rice, beans, and hummus; although these still lack vitamin B12, which is plentiful in meat. It is essential for growth, energy, nerves, and healthy blood, so you should take it as a supplement.

Opposite page: The view from beyond, preparing to fly my foil at home on Kauai.

DRINK H²O

Hydration is the key to a healthy life. Water is central to almost every function of the human body. About 65 percent of our body is made of water, starting with the brain, where healthy hydration is required to manufacture hormones and neurotransmitters. Water is equally critical for the entire body to function efficiently in the processes of blood circulation, metabolism, temperature regulation, waste removal and detoxification. Dehydration can cause headaches, bad breath, sugar cravings, aching joints, dry skin, constipation, and muscle cramps.

Water is widely available, cheap, calorie-free, and the most important thing you can put in your body. I drink more water than most, but as a rough guide, you should aim to drink half your body weight (in pounds) in ounces per day. So if you weigh 200 pounds, you should take in 100 ounces of water per day—and remember that other fluid intake does not count as part of this quota. Thirst level and the color of your urine are good indicators of being hydrated. You would like your urine to be a light-yellow color. Children are a little different because thirst indicators are underdeveloped, so they are at a higher risk for dehydration. It is also worth noting that hunger (especially sugar cravings) can be an indicator that one is moving toward dehydration, and it's important to act immediately when these symptoms show themselves.

The first thing I do in the morning—before I eat or drink anything, even my coffee—is drink a large glass of water. If you are unsure of the nutritional value of your water, you can add some Himalayan pink salt (this contains the same 84 trace minerals and elements that are found in the human body).

> **"I RECOMMEND REFILLING A STAINLESS-STEEL CANTEEN, AND HOPEFULLY YOU WILL START TO NOTICE THAT IT BECOMES A HABIT TO KEEP A BOTTLE OF WATER WITH YOU IN THE CAR OR AT YOUR DESK."**

A water filter on your home supply is a great idea, although we favor a reverse osmosis machine, which removes contaminants such as arsenic, nitrates, sodium, copper, lead, some organic chemicals, and the municipal additive fluoride. Nothing beats water, however, real coconut water is the next best way to get hydrated. Definitely avoid all drinks with added sugar, and if you need electrolytes, just add them to water to forgo all the sugar and additives in sports drinks.

Opposite page: In the absence of my ice bath, a cold shower is a great way for your body to recover from exercise.

THE RIGHT CARBOHYDRATES

While we can survive without sugar, it would be much more difficult to eliminate carbohydrates entirely from our diet. They are the sugars, starches, and fibers found in fruits, grains, vegetables, and milk products—the body's main source of energy. They are called carbohydrates because, at the molecular level, they contain carbon, hydrogen, and oxygen atoms.

> **THE SIMPLE CARBOHYDRATES, THOSE IN REFINED WHITE SUGAR AND PROCESSED FOOD AND DRINK, NEED TO BE AVOIDED. THEY ARE EMPTY OF CALORIES AND ONLY PROVIDE A BLOOD-SUGAR JOLT, FOLLOWED BY AN ENERGY CRASH.**

Vegetables are abundant in carbohydrates; it's not just pasta and potatoes that are unjustly labelled the dreaded "carbs!" We can get plenty of energy from vegetables, especially if we are consuming healthy fats. Some of my favorite and most-powerful carbs are the following: Jackfruit, one of the weirdest super-fruits that has a breadlike texture and is an amazing source of carbohydrates, as well as plant based proteins, vitamins, amino acids and minerals. Sweet potatoes are another incredible powerhouse, rich in simple starches and complex carbohydrates, also benefiting from naturally occurring sugars that raise insulin levels. Taro is a popular root in Hawaii and one of the finest sources of dietary fiber, with slow-digesting complex carbs that give you long-lasting energy levels.

Studies show that if we are hydrated and eat enough healthy fat, we can get enough carbohydrates from our food. Everyone is different. I like the idea of eating carbs as half of my diet one week, then a little less, and then at about 65 percent of my caloric intake. You will find out which percentage works best for you and how you convert food to energy. Take time out to notice if you feel sleepy after lunch, how your elimination is, and even your sleep. We are all unique, so take time to answer this question for yourself.

Opposite page: One of the most mesmerizing views from our home on Kauai, which I like to call "Jurassic Park."

LAIRD SUPERFOOD

Our Superfood company is one of the latest additions in the evolution of our health and fitness portfolio. As a longtime coffee lover, I've always tinkered with different variants and recipes. Finally, I had to develop some convenient products to enhance the whole coffee experience and take the energy-boosting properties to the next level. We think of Superfood as an "alternative energy" company, offering optimal performance through healthy living. Superfood is focused on providing our customers with the strongest and most-sustained all-natural energy source available in the marketplace today. The creamers optimize the effects of caffeine by combining medium-chain triglycerides derived from coconut products and a variety of natural oils, as well as Aquamin (a nutrient-rich calcified sea algae) with coffee. This unique set of all-natural ingredients delivers a slow release of energy that can last up to four or five hours. I use it on a daily basis to power myself through the most demanding surf sessions on the planet. Our Superfood Creamers are extremely versatile, and as you can see in this book, you can use them effectively in smoothies and food recipes alike.

Whether you are a high-performance athlete seeking an all-natural energy advantage, a professional looking to work more effectively at the office, or a concerned mom desiring an all-natural alternative to traditionally chemical-laden sweeteners and creamers, our Superfood Creamers will provide the natural boost you need to keep functioning at a high level. Our Superfood product line is expanding into a variety of different food and drink categories. A great example is Hydrate, our all-natural alternative to traditionally sugar-laden sports drinks. Hydrate contains only two ingredients, both all-natural, that together provide the desired level of electrolytes and calcium to improve hydration and sustain performance. Whether it be the creamers, hydration enhancers, or other unique food additives, every single Superfood product is specifically designed to increase energy levels, enhance daily performance, and improve the nutritional density of one's diet in an all-natural and health-focused fashion.

Please visit our online shop at www.lairdsuperfood.com and try some of our unique products in your food and drink recipes.

Opposite page: Our Superfood products enhance your coffee and transform a smoothie.

RECIPE INDEX

THIRD SESSION

Banyans Halibut with Macadamia Nut Crust & Riced Broccoli with Turmeric
   Coconut Sauce, 110-111

Bondi Gluten-Free Breaded Tilapia with Zesty Arugula, Radish & Cucumber Salad, 121

Chicama Beef Stir-Fry with Onion, Bell Peppers, Garlic & Hand-made Oven Fries, 114

Grand Haven Bison Chili with Homemade Corn Tortilla Chips, 118

Green Bowl Chicken Curry with Green Beans, Bell Peppers & Basil, 113

Honky's Squash Koktas in Masala Curry Sauce, 97

Kamala Grilled Salmon with Cucumber & Red Onion Salsa with Wild Rice &
   Sweet Chili Dipping Sauce, 109

Keramas Snapper with Stir-fried Ginger, Carrot, Asparagus & Broccolini, 91

La Chapelle Chicken Cassoulet with Olive, Sausage, Parma, Rosemary, Garlic,
   Cannellini Beans & Fennel, 117

La Torche Roasted Chicken with Lemon, Rosemary, Sautéed Brussels Sprouts
   & Smashed Celery Root, 88-89

Little Dume Grilled T-Bone Steak & Roasted Red Potatoes, Radishes
   with Fennel & Lemon Butter Sauce, 106

Point Venus Coconut Curried Mussels with Lime and Garlic, 87

Supertubos Paella with Chicken, Chorizo, Clams & Mussels, 99

Temae Spiny Lobster with Lemon Butter & Sautéed Sweet Potatoes, 100

Trigg Point Sautéed Turkey Meatballs with Tomato & Onion Sauce
   on Spaghetti Squash, 103

Waimea Ahi Poke with Sweet Onion, Avocado, Seaweed & Sesame with Wild Rice, 84

Yumuri BBQ Sea Bass with Roasted Sweet Potatoes & Okra with Salsa Verde, 94-95

FOURTH SESSION

Haiku Banana Bread with Grill Pineapple, Yogurt & Mint, 126

Higgins Mixed-Berry Cobbler, 129

Kahalu'u Chilled Chocolate Avocado Mousse Cake, 125

Shipwrecks Banana Rolled in Granola Fried in Honey & Cinnamon, 130

INGREDIENTS INDEX

C

CABBAGE

Uchiumi Point Steak Salad with Edamame, Greens & Orange Sesame Dressing, 62

CACAO POWDER

Kahalu'u Chilled Chocolate Avocado Mousse Cake, 125

Laird's Coffee & Cacao Smoothie, 45

CAPERS

Yumuri BBQ Sea Bass with Roasted Sweet Potatoes & Okra with Salsa Verde, 94

CARROTS

Keramas Snapper with Stir-fried Ginger, Carrot, Asparagus & Broccolini, 91

Mundaka Tomato, Carrot & Turmeric Bisque Soup, 48

Shimei Bay Omelet with Stir-fried Vegetables in Sesame Oil with Noodles, 26

CASHEW BUTTER

Kahalu'u Chilled Chocolate Avocado Mousse Cake, 125

Laird's Beet & Berry Smoothie, 42

CASHEWS

Honky's Squash Koftas in Masala Curry Sauce, 97

Superbank Chopped Chicken, Bacon, Egg, Spinach & Kale Salad, Asian Pear, Avocado, Cashew & Raisins with Curry Dressing, 78

CAULIFLOWER

Banyans Halibut with Macadamia Nut Crust & Riced Broccoli with Turmeric Coconut Sauce, 110-111

CAYENNE PEPPER

Honky's Squash Koftas in Masala Curry Sauce, 97

Les Cavaliers Salmon, Spinach & Sun-Dried Tomato Crêpes, 38-39

CELERY

La Torche Roasted Chicken with Lemon, Rosemary, Sautéed Brussels Sprouts & Smashed Celery Root, 88

CHEESE, GOAT

Kalo Nero Grilled Fig & Prosciutto Salad, 71

Raglan Quinoa Salad with Grilled Corn, Mango, Tomatoes, Avocado & Goat Cheese, 77

CHEESE, PARMESAN

Bondi Gluten-Free Breaded Tilapia with Zesty Arugula, Radish & Cucumber Salad, 121

Les Cavaliers Salmon, Spinach & Sun-Dried Tomato Crêpes, 38-39

Marinaretti Zucchini Soup, 51

Shipwrecks Banana Rolled in Granola Fried in Honey & Cinnamon, 130

CHIA SEEDS

Laird's Beet & Berry Smoothie, 42

CHICKEN

Green Bowl Chicken Curry with Green Beans, Bell Peppers & Basil, 113

La Chapelle Chicken Cassoulet with Olive, Sausage, Parma, Rosemary, Garlic, Cannellini Beans & Fennel, 117

La Torche Roasted Chicken with Lemon, Rosemary, Sautéed Brussels Sprouts & Smashed Celery Root, 88

Superbank Chopped Chicken, Bacon, Egg, Spinach & Kale Salad, Asian Pear, Avocado, Cashew & Raisins with Curry Dressing, 78

Supertubos Paella with Chicken, Chorizo, Clams & Mussels, 99

CHICKPEAS

Ipanema Fresh Vegetable & Coconut Curry with Wild Rice, 74

CHILES DE ARBOL

Playa Grande Grilled Pork Burger with Chimichurri Sauce & Sweet Potato Fries, 56

CHILIS, GREEN

Green Bowl Chicken Curry with Green Beans, Bell Peppers & Basil, 113

Honky's Squash Koftas in Masala Curry Sauce, 97

CHILIS, RED HOT

Anchor Point Shakshuka, Tomatoes, Peppers, Artichokes and Smoked Paprika with Eggs, 30

Chesterman Gluten-Free Toast, Bacon, Roasted Cherry Tomatoes & Guacamole, 41

Hanalei Bowl Chilled Avocado Soup with Summer Salsa, 55

La Torche Roasted Chicken with Lemon, Rosemary, Sautéed Brussels Sprouts & Smashed Celery Root, 88

Papara Marinated Squid with Chili Oil & Fresh Rosemary Served on Arugula Salad, 81

Shimei Bay Omelet with Stir-fried Vegetables in Sesame Oil with Noodles, 26

CHIVES

Banyans Halibut with Macadamia Nut Crust & Riced Broccoli with Turmeric Coconut Sauce, 110-111

Les Cavaliers Salmon, Spinach & Sun-Dried Tomato Crêpes, 38-39

Mundaka Tomato, Carrot & Turmeric Bisque Soup, 48

Raglan Quinoa Salad with Grilled Corn, Mango, Tomatoes, Avocado & Goat Cheese, 77

CHOCOLATE CHIPS

Kahalu'u Chilled Chocolate Avocado Mousse Cake, 125

CHORIZO

Escondido Breakfast Burrito with Chorizo, Eggs, Beans, Avocado & Pico de Gallo, 20

Playa Grande Grilled Pork Burger with Chimichurri Sauce & Sweet Potato Fries, 56

Supertubos Paella with Chicken, Chorizo, Clams & Mussels, 99

CILANTRO

Anchor Point Shakshuka, Tomatoes, Peppers, Artichokes and Smoked Paprika with Eggs, 30

Cloudbreak Seared Tuna with
Crunchy Salad with Red Potatoes
& Lemon, 61

Escondido Breakfast Burrito with
Chorizo, Eggs, Beans, Avocado &
Pico de Gallo, 20

First Point Grilled Tilapia Tacos
with Kiwi, Pomegranate & Lime
Salsa with Gluten-Free Tortillas, 65

Chesterman Gluten-Free Toast,
Bacon, Roasted Cherry Tomatoes
& Guacamole, 41

Grand Haven Bison Chili with
Homemade Corn Tortilla Chips, 118

Green Bowl Chicken Curry
with Green Beans, Bell Peppers &
Basil, 113

Hanalei Bowl Chilled Avocado
Soup with Summer Salsa, 55

Honky's Squash Koftas in Masala
Curry Sauce, 97

Ipanema Fresh Vegetable &
Coconut Curry with Wild Rice, 74

Kamala Grilled Salmon with
Cucumber & Red Onion Salsa
with Wild Rice & Sweet Chili
Dipping Sauce, 109

Point Venus Coconut Curried
Mussels with Lime and Garlic, 87

Raglan Quinoa Salad with Grilled
Corn, Mango, Tomatoes,
Avocado & Goat Cheese, 77

Shimei Bay Omelet with Stir-fried
Vegetables in Sesame Oil
with Noodles, 26

CINNAMON

Banyans Halibut with Macadamia
Nut Crust & Riced Broccoli with
Turmeric Coconut Sauce, 110-111

Higgins Mixed-Berry Cobbler, 129

Kalo Nero Grilled Fig & Prosciutto
Salad, 71

Laird's Banana & Turmeric
Smoothie, 42

Laird's Coffee & Cacao Smoothie, 45

Shipwrecks Banana Rolled in
Granola Fried in Honey &
Cinnamon, 130

CLAMS

Supertubos Paella with Chicken,
Chorizo, Clams & Mussels, 99

COCONUT CREAM

Ipanema Fresh Vegetable &
Coconut Curry with Wild Rice, 74

Coconut milk. See milk, coconut.

Coconut sugar. See sugar, coconut.

COFFEE

Half Moon Coffee and Cacao
Granola with Natural Yogurt &
Roasted Strawberries, 34

Laird's Coffee & Cacao Smoothie, 45

CORIANDER

Grand Haven Bison Chili with
Homemade Corn Tortilla Chips, 118

Green Bowl Chicken Curry with
Green Beans, Bell Peppers & Basil, 113

Honky's Squash Koftas in Masala
Curry Sauce, 97

Keramas Snapper with Stir-fried
Ginger, Carrot, Asparagus &
Broccolini, 91

CORIANDER SEEDS

Cloudbreak Seared Tuna with
Crunchy Salad with Red Potatoes
& Lemon, 61

CORN

Raglan Quinoa Salad with Grilled
Corn, Mango, Tomatoes,
Avocado & Goat Cheese, 77

CREAMER

Laird's Beet & Berry Smoothie, 42

Laird's Lean Green Smoothie, 45

Lusty Glaze Blended Porridge with
Blueberries and Pumpkin Seeds, 16

Marinaretti Zucchini Soup, 51

Mullaghmore Beet & Apple Soup, 52

CREAMER, CACAO

Half Moon Coffee and Cacao
Granola with Natural Yogurt &
Roasted Strawberries, 34

Kahalu'u Chilled Chocolate
Avocado Mousse Cake, 125

Laird's Coffee & Cacao Smoothie, 45

CREAMER, TURMERIC

Banyans Halibut with Macadamia
Nut Crust & Riced Broccoli with
Turmeric Coconut Sauce, 110-111

Honky's Squash Koftas in Masala
Curry Sauce, 97

Keramas Snapper with Stir-fried
Ginger, Carrot, Asparagus &
Broccolini, 91

Laird's Banana & Turmeric
Smoothie, 42

Mundaka Tomato, Carrot &
Turmeric Bisque Soup, 48

CROUTONS

Mundaka Tomato, Carrot &
Turmeric Bisque Soup, 48

CUCUMBER

Bondi Gluten-Free Breaded Tilapia
with Zesty Arugula, Radish &
Cucumber Salad, 121

Cloudbreak Seared Tuna with
Crunchy Salad with Red Potatoes
& Lemon, 61

Hanalei Bowl Chilled Avocado
Soup with Summer Salsa, 55

Kamala Grilled Salmon with
Cucumber & Red Onion Salsa
with Wild Rice, 109

CUMIN

Anchor Point Shakshuka,
Tomatoes, Peppers, Artichokes
and Smoked Paprika with Eggs, 30

Ditch Plains Green Pancakes with
Onions, Chili & Spinach, 23

Grand Haven Bison Chili with
Homemade Corn Tortilla Chips, 118

Green Bowl Chicken Curry with
Green Beans, Bell Peppers & Basil, 113

Honky's Squash Koftas in Masala
Curry Sauce, 97

Playa Grande Grilled Pork Burger
with Chimichurri Sauce & Sweet
Potato Fries, 56

Wild Coast Sausage with Scrambled
Eggs, Cherry Tomatoes, Spinach
and Wild Rice, 19

CURRY PASTE, GREEN

Point Venus Coconut Curried
Mussels with Lime and Garlic, 87

CURRY POWDER

Superbank Chopped Chicken,
Bacon, Egg, Spinach & Kale Salad,
Asian Pear, Avocado, Cashew &
Raisins with Curry Dressing, 78

D

DILL

Mullaghmore Beet & Apple Soup, 52

Yumuri BBQ Sea Bass with Roasted
Sweet Potatoes & Okra with
Salsa Verde, 94

E

EDAMAME BEANS

Uchiumi Point Steak Salad with
Edamame, Greens & Orange
Sesame Dressing, 62

EGGPLANT

Ipanema Fresh Vegetable &
Coconut Curry with Wild Rice, 74

EGGS

Aleutian Wild Salmon and Quinoa
Burger with Pesto and Two Eggs, 33

Anchor Point Shakshuka,
Tomatoes, Peppers, Artichokes
and Smoked Paprika with Eggs, 30

Banyans Halibut with Macadamia
Nut Crust & Riced Broccoli with
Turmeric Coconut Sauce, 110-111

Ditch Plains Green Pancakes with
Onions, Chili & Spinach, 23

Escondido Breakfast Burrito with
Chorizo, Eggs, Beans, Avocado &
Pico de Gallo, 20

Haiku Banana Bread with Grilled
Pineapple, Yogurt & Mint, 126

Nijima Mixed Mushroom Ragout
with Poached Egg, 29

Shimei Bay Omelet with Stir-fried
Vegetables in Sesame Oil with
Noodles, 26

Superbank Chopped Chicken,
Bacon, Egg, Spinach & Kale Salad,
Asian Pear, Avocado, Cashew &
Raisins with Curry Dressing, 78

Trigg Point Sautéed Turkey
Meatballs with Tomato & Onion
Sauce on Spaghetti Squash, 103

Wild Coast Sausage with Scrambled
Eggs, Cherry Tomatoes, Spinach
and Wild Rice, 19

ESPRESSO

Laird's Coffee & Cacao Smoothie, 45

F

FENNEL

La Chapelle Chicken Cassoulet
with Olive, Sausage, Parma,
Rosemary, Garlic, Cannellini
Beans & Fennel,117

Little Dume Grilled T-Bone Steak
with Roasted Red Potatoes,
Radishes with Fennel & Lemon
Butter Sauce, 106

FIGS

Kalo Nero Grilled Fig & Prosciutto
Salad, 71

FISH SAUCE

Green Bowl Chicken Curry with
Green Beans, Bell Peppers & Basil, 113

Kamala Grilled Salmon with
Cucumber & Red Onion Salsa
with Wild Rice & Sweet Chili
Dipping Sauce, 109

Point Venus Coconut Curried
Mussels with Lime and Garlic, 87

FLAXSEED MEAL

Laird's Coffee & Cacao Smoothie, 45

FLAXSEEDS

Lusty Glaze Blended Porridge with
Blueberries and Pumpkin Seeds, 16

FLOUR

Ditch Plains Green Pancakes with
Onions, Chili & Spinach, 23

Haiku Banana Bread with Grilled
Pineapple, Yogurt & Mint, 126

Honky's Squash Koftas in Masala
Curry Sauce, 97

Mundaka Tomato, Carrot &
Turmeric Bisque Soup, 48

Nijima Mixed Mushroom Ragout
with Poached Egg, 29

Trigg Point Sautéed Turkey
Meatballs with Tomato & Onion
Sauce on Spaghetti Squash, 103

FLOUR, ALMOND

Higgins Mixed-Berry Cobbler, 129

FLOUR, TAPIOCA

Higgins Mixed-Berry Cobbler, 129

FRISÉE

Kalo Nero Grilled Fig & Prosciutto
Salad, 71

FRUITS, DRIED

Half Moon Coffee and Cacao
Granola with Natural Yogurt &
Roasted Strawberries, 34

G

GARAM MARSALA

Honky's Squash Koftas in Masala
Curry Sauce, 97

GARLIC

Aleutian Wild Salmon and Quinoa
Burger with Pesto and Two Eggs, 33

Anchor Point Shakshuka,
Tomatoes, Peppers, Artichokes
and Smoked Paprika with Eggs, 30

Banyans Halibut with Macadamia
Nut Crust & Riced Broccoli wit
Turmeric Coconut Sauce, 110-111

Bondi Gluten-Free Breaded Tilapia
with Zesty Arugula, Radish &
Cucumber Salad, 121

Chicama Beef Stir-Fry with Onion,
Bell Peppers, Garlic & Hand-made
Oven Fries, 114

Cloudbreak Seared Tuna with
Crunchy Salad with Red Potatoes
& Lemon, 61

Chesterman Gluten-Free Toast,
Bacon, Roasted Cherry Tomatoes
& Guacamole, 41

Grand Haven Bison Chili
with Homemade Corn Tortilla
Chips, 118

Bondi Gluten-Free Breaded Tilapia
with Zesty Arugula, Radish &
Cucumber Salad, 121
Cloudbreak Seared Tuna with
Crunchy Salad with Red Potatoes
& Lemon, 61
Hanalei Bowl Chilled Avocado
Soup with Summer Salsa, 55
Imsouane Bay Spicy Shrimp with
Orange & Seasonal Quinoa Salad, 66
Les Cavaliers Salmon, Spinach &
Sun-Dried Tomato Crêpes, 38-39
Little Dume Grilled T-Bone
Steak with Roasted Red Potatoes,
Radishes with Fennel & Lemon
Butter Sauce, 106
Papara Marinated Squid with Chili
Oil & Fresh Rosemary Served on
Arugula Salad, 81
Superbank Chopped Chicken,
Bacon, Egg, Spinach & Kale Salad,
Asian Pear, Avocado, Cashew &
Raisins with Curry Dressing, 78
Supertubos Paella with Chicken,
Chorizo, Clams & Mussels, 99
Temae Spiny Lobster with Lemon
Butter & Sautéed Sweet Potatoes, 100

LEMONGRASS

Green Bowl Chicken Curry with
Green Beans, Bell Peppers
& Basil, 113
Point Venus Coconut Curried
Mussels with Lime and Garlic, 87

LEMONS

Aleutian Wild Salmon and Quinoa
Burger with Pesto and Two Eggs, 33
Bondi Gluten-Free Breaded Tilapia
with Zesty Arugula, Radish
& Cucumber Salad, 121
Cloudbreak Seared Tuna with
Crunchy Salad with Red Potatoes
& Lemon, 61
Ditch Plains Green Pancakes with
Onions, Chili & Spinach, 23
Keramas Snapper with Stir-fried
Ginger, Carrot, Asparagus &
Broccolini, 91

La Chapelle Chicken Cassoulet
with Olive, Sausage, Parma,
Rosemary, Garlic, Cannellini
Beans & Fennel, 117
La Torche Roasted Chicken
with Lemon, Rosemary, Sautéed
Brussels Sprouts & Smashed
Celery Root, 88
Temae Spiny Lobster with Lemon
Butter & Sautéed Sweet Potatoes, 100
Yumuri BBQ Sea Bass with Roasted
Sweet Potatoes & Okra with Salsa
Verde, 94

LETTUCE, ICEBERG

Cloudbreak Seared Tuna with
Crunchy Salad with Red Potatoes
& Lemon, 61

LIME JUICE

Escondido Breakfast Burrito with
Chorizo, Eggs, Beans, Avocado &
Pico de Gallo, 20
Chesterman Gluten-Free Toast,
Bacon, Roasted Cherry Tomatoes
& Guacamole, 41
Laird's Banana & Turmeric
Smoothie, 42
Raglan Quinoa Salad with Grilled
Corn, Mango, Tomatoes,
Avocado & Goat Cheese, 77
Yumuri BBQ Sea Bass with Roasted
Sweet Potatoes & Okra with Salsa
Verde, 94

LIMES

Green Bowl Chicken Curry
with Green Beans, Bell Peppers
& Basil, 113
Keramas Snapper with Stir-fried
Ginger, Carrot, Asparagus &
Broccolini, 91
Point Venus Coconut Curried
Mussels with Lime and Garlic, 87

LOBSTERS

Temae Spiny Lobster with
Lemon Butter & Sautéed Sweet
Potatoes, 100

M

MACADAMIA NUTS

Banyans Halibut with Macadamia
Nut Crust & Riced Broccoli with
Turmeric Coconut Sauce, 110-111
Keramas Snapper with Stir-fried
Ginger, Carrot, Asparagus &
Broccolini, 91

MANGO

Raglan Quinoa Salad with Grilled
Corn, Mango, Tomatoes,
Avocado & Goat Cheese, 77

MAPLE SYRUP

Higgins Mixed-Berry Cobbler, 129
Kahalu'u Chilled Chocolate
Avocado Mousse Cake, 125
Little Dume Grilled T-Bone Steak
with Red Potatoes, Radishes with
Fennel & Lemon Butter Sauce, 106

MASA HARINA

Grand Haven Bison Chili
with Homemade Corn Tortilla
Chips, 118

MEAL POWDER

Laird's Lean Green Smoothie, 45

MILK

Ditch Plains Green Pancakes with
Onions, Chili & Spinach, 23
Lusty Glaze Blended Porridge with
Blueberries and Pumpkin Seeds, 16

MILK, ALMOND

Higgins Mixed-Berry Cobbler, 129
Kahalu'u Chilled Chocolate
Avocado Mousse Cake, 125
Laird's Banana & Turmeric
Smoothie, 42
Laird's Beet & Berry Smoothie, 42
Les Cavaliers Salmon, Spinach &
Sun-Dried Tomato Crêpes, 38-39

MILK, COCONUT

Banyans Halibut with Macadamia
Nut Crust & Riced Broccoli with
Turmeric Coconut Sauce, 110-111
Green Bowl Chicken Curry with
Green Beans, Bell Peppers & Basil, 113
Haiku Banana Bread with Grilled
Pineapple, Yogurt & Mint, 126

Trigg Point Sautéed Turkey
Meatballs with Tomato & Onion
Sauce on Spaghetti Squash, 103
Yumuri BBQ Sea Bass with Roasted
Sweet Potatoes & Okra with Salsa
Verde, 94

OIL, SESAME
Kamala Grilled Salmon with
Cucumber & Red Onion Salsa
with Wild Rice & Sweet Chili
Dipping Sauce, 109
Shimei Bay Omelet with Stir-fried
Vegetables in Sesame Oil with
Noodles, 26
Uchiumi Point Steak Salad with
Edamame, Greens & Orange
Sesame Dressing, 62
Waimea Ahi Poke with Sweet
Onion, Avocado, Seaweed &
Sesame with Wild Rice, 84

OIL, VEGETABLE
Chicama Beef Stir-Fry with Onion,
Bell Peppers, Garlic & Hand-made
Oven Fries, 114
Escondido Breakfast Burrito with
Chorizo, Eggs, Beans, Avocado
& Pico de Gallo, 20
Honky's Squash Koftas in Masala
Curry Sauce, 97
Keramas Snapper with Stir-fried
Ginger, Carrot, Asparagus &
Broccolini, 91
Shimei Bay Omelet with Stir-fried
Vegetables in Sesame Oil with, 26
Wild Coast Sausage with Scrambled
Eggs, Cherry Tomatoes, Spinach
and Wild Rice, 19

OKRA
Yumuri BBQ Sea Bass with Roasted
Sweet Potatoes & Okra with Salsa
Verde, 94

OLIVES
Anchor Point Shakshuka,
Tomatoes, Peppers, Artichokes
and Smoked Paprika with Eggs, 30
Cloudbreak Seared Tuna with
Crunchy Salad with Red Potatoes
& Lemon, 61

ONIONS
Anchor Point Shakshuka,
Tomatoes, Peppers, Artichokes
and Smoked Paprika with Eggs, 30
Grand Haven Bison Chili with
Homemade Corn Tortilla Chips, 118
Mullaghmore Beet & Apple Soup, 52
Mundaka Tomato, Carrot &
Turmeric Bisque Soup, 48
Nijima Mixed Mushroom Ragout
with Poached Egg, 29
Supertubos Paella with Chicken,
Chorizo, Clams & Mussels, 99
Waimea Ahi Poke with Sweet
Onion, Avocado, Seaweed &
Sesame with Wild Rice, 84

ONIONS, GREEN
Aleutian Wild Salmon and Quinoa
Burger with Pesto and Two Eggs, 33
Ditch Plains Green Pancakes with
Onions, Chili & Spinach, 23
First Point Grilled Tilapia Tacos
with Kiwi, Pomegranate & Lime
Salsa with Gluten-Free Tortillas, 65
Grand Haven Bison Chili
with Homemade Corn Tortilla
Chips, 118
Imsouane Bay Spicy Shrimp with
Orange & Seasonal Quinoa Salad, 66
Mundaka Tomato, Carrot &
Turmeric Bisque Soup, 48
Supertubos Paella with Chicken,
Chorizo, Clams & Mussels, 99
Uchiumi Point Steak Salad with
Edamame, Greens & Orange
Sesame Dressing, 62
Wild Coast Sausage with Scrambled
Eggs, Cherry Tomatoes, Spinach
and Wild Rice, 19

ONIONS, RED
Chicama Beef Stir-Fry with Onion,
Bell Peppers, Garlic & Hand-made
Oven Fries, 114
Escondido Breakfast Burrito with
Chorizo, Eggs, Beans, Avocado &
Pico de Gallo, 20
Chesterman Gluten-Free Toast,
Bacon, Roasted Cherry Tomatoes
& Guacamole, 41

Hanalei Bowl Chilled Avocado
Soup with Summer Salsa, 55
Ipanema Fresh Vegetable &
Coconut Curry with Wild Rice, 74
Kamala Grilled Salmon with
Cucumber & Red Onion Salsa
with Wild Rice & Sweet Chili
Dipping Sauce, 109

ONIONS, SPRING
Shimei Bay Omelet with Stir-fried
Vegetables in Sesame Oil
with Noodles, 26

ONIONS, YELLOW
Banyans Halibut with Macadamia
Nut Crust & Riced Broccoli with
Turmeric Coconut Sauce, 110-111
Honky's Squash Koftas in Masala
Curry Sauce, 97
Point Venus Coconut Curried
Mussels with Lime and Garlic, 87
Trigg Point Sautéed Turkey
Meatballs with Tomato & Onion
Sauce on Spaghetti Squash, 103

ORANGE JUICE
Uchiumi Point Steak Salad with
Edamame, Greens & Orange
Sesame Dressing, 62

OREGANO
Grand Haven Bison Chili
with Homemade Corn Tortilla
Chips, 118
Trigg Point Sautéed Turkey
Meatballs with Tomato & Onion
Sauce on Spaghetti Squash, 103

P

PANCETTA
La Torche Roasted Chicken
with Lemon, Rosemary, Sautéed
Brussels Sprouts & Smashed
Celery Root, 88

PAPRIKA
Anchor Point Shakshuka,
Tomatoes, Peppers, Artichokes
and Smoked Paprika with Eggs, 30
Bondi Gluten-Free Breaded Tilapia
with Zesty Arugula, Radish &
Cucumber Salad, 121

Grand Haven Bison Chili
with Homemade Corn Tortilla
Chips, 118
Imsouane Bay Spicy Shrimp with
Orange & Seasonal Quinoa Salad, 66
Wild Coast Sausage with Scrambled
Eggs, Cherry Tomatoes, Spinach
and Wild Rice, 19

PARSLEY

Aleutian Wild Salmon and Quinoa
Burger with Pesto and Two Eggs, 33
Anchor Point Shakshuka,
Tomatoes, Peppers, Artichokes
and Smoked Paprika with Eggs, 30
Bondi Gluten-Free Breaded Tilapia
with Zesty Arugula, Radish
& Cucumber Salad, 121
Chicama Beef Stir-Fry with Onion,
Bell Peppers, Garlic & Hand-made
Oven Fries, 114
Ditch Plains Green Pancakes with
Onions, Chili & Spinach, 23
Marinaretti Zucchini Soup, 51
Nijima Mixed Mushroom Ragout
with Poached Egg, 29
Playa Grande Grilled Pork Burger
with Chimichurri Sauce & Sweet
Potato Fries, 56
Supertubos Paella with Chicken,
Chorizo, Clams & Mussels, 99
Temae Spiny Lobster with Lemon
Butter & Sautéed Sweet Potatoes, 100
Trigg Point Sautéed Turkey
Meatballs with Tomato & Onion
Sauce on Spaghetti Squash, 103
Yumuri BBQ Sea Bass with Roasted
Sweet Potatoes & Okra with Salsa
Verde, 94

PEARS

Superbank Chopped Chicken,
Bacon, Egg, Spinach & Kale Salad,
Asian Pear, Avocado, Cashew &
Raisins with Curry Dressing, 78

PEAS

Supertubos Paella with Chicken,
Chorizo, Clams & Mussels, 99

PEAS, SNOW

Keramas Snapper with Stir-fried
Ginger, Carrot, Asparagus &
Broccolini, 91

PECANS

Half Moon Coffee and Cacao
Granola with Natural Yogurt
& Roasted Strawberries, 34
Kahalu'u Chilled Chocolate
Avocado Mousse Cake, 125

PEPPERCORNS

La Chapelle Chicken Cassoulet
with Olive, Sausage, Parma,
Rosemary, Garlic, Cannellini
Beans & Fennel, 117

PEPPERS, GREEN BELL

Chicama Beef Stir-Fry with
Onion, Bell Peppers, Garlic
& and-made Oven Fries, 114

PEPPERS, JALAPEÑO

Ditch Plains Green Pancakes with
Onions, Chili & Spinach, 23
Escondido Breakfast Burrito with
Chorizo, Eggs, Beans, Avocado
& Pico de Gallo, 20
First Point Grilled Tilapia Tacos
with Kiwi, Pomegranate & Lime
Salsa with Gluten-Free Tortillas, 65

PEPPERS, RED BELL

Chicama Beef Stir-Fry with
Onion, Bell Peppers, Garlic &
Hand-made Oven Fries, 114
Green Bowl Chicken Curry
with Green Beans, Bell Peppers
& Basil, 113
Imsouane Bay Spicy Shrimp with
Orange & Seasonal Quinoa Salad, 66
Ipanema Fresh Vegetable &
Coconut Curry with Wild Rice, 74
Supertubos Paella with Chicken,
Chorizo, Clams & Mussels, 99
Uchiumi Point Steak Salad with
Edamame, Greens & Orange
Sesame Dressing, 62

PEPPERS, RED CHILI

Ipanema Fresh Vegetable &
Coconut Curry with Wild Rice, 74

Kamala Grilled Salmon with
Cucumber & Red Onion Salsa
with Wild Rice & Sweet Chili
Dipping Sauce, 109

PEPPERS, YELLOW BELL

Hanalei Bowl Chilled Avocado
Soup with Summer Salsa, 55
Imsouane Bay Spicy Shrimp with
Orange & Seasonal Quinoa Salad, 66

PINE NUTS

Aleutian Wild Salmon and Quinoa
Burger with Pesto and Two Eggs, 33

PINEAPPLES

Haiku Banana Bread with Grilled
Pineapple, Yogurt & Mint, 126
Laird's Banana & Turmeric
Smoothie, 42

PISTACHIOS

Kalo Nero Grilled Fig & Prosciutto
Salad, 71

POMEGRANATE SEEDS

First Point Grilled Tilapia Tacos
with Kiwi, Pomegranate & Lime
Salsa with Gluten-Free Tortillas, 65
Imsouane Bay Spicy Shrimp with
Orange & Seasonal Quinoa Salad, 66

PORK

Playa Grande Grilled Pork Burger
with Chimichurri Sauce & Sweet
Potato Fries, 56

POTATOES

Chicama Beef Stir-Fry with Onion,
Bell Peppers, Garlic & Hand-made
Oven Fries, 114
Cloudbreak Seared Tuna with
Crunchy Salad with Red Potatoes
& Lemon, 61
Little Dume Grilled T-Bone
Steak with Roasted Red Potatoes,
Radishes with Fennel & Lemon
Butter Sauce, 106

PROSCIUTTO

Kalo Nero Grilled Fig & Prosciutto
Salad, 71

PUMPKIN SEEDS

Lusty Glaze Blended Porridge with
Blueberries and Pumpkin Seeds, 16

Q

QUINOA
Aleutian Wild Salmon and Quinoa Burger with Pesto and Two Eggs, 33

Imsouane Bay Spicy Shrimp with Orange & Seasonal Quinoa Salad, 66

Lusty Glaze Blended Porridge with Blueberries and Pumpkin Seeds, 16

Raglan Quinoa Salad with Grilled Corn, Mango, Tomatoes, Avocado & Goat Cheese, 77

R

RADISHES
Bondi Gluten-Free Breaded Tilapia with Zesty Arugula, Radish & Cucumber Salad, 121

Little Dume Grilled T-Bone Steak with Roasted Red Potatoes, Radishes with Fennel & Lemon Butter Sauce, 106

RAISINS
Superbank Chopped Chicken, Bacon, Egg, Spinach & Kale Salad, Asian Pear, Avocado, Cashew & Raisins with Curry Dressing, 78

RASPBERRIES
Higgins Mixed-Berry Cobbler, 129

Laird's Beet & Berry Smoothie, 42

RED PEPPER FLAKES
Bondi Gluten-Free Breaded Tilapia with Zesty Arugula, Radish & Cucumber Salad, 121

Cloudbreak Seared Tuna with Crunchy Salad with Red Potatoes & Lemon, 61

Grand Haven Bison Chili with Homemade Corn Tortilla Chips, 118

Kamala Grilled Salmon with Cucumber & Red Onion Salsa with Wild Rice & Sweet Chili Dipping Sauce, 109

La Torche Roasted Chicken with Lemon, Rosemary, Sautéed Brussels Sprouts & Smashed Celery Root, 88

Waimea Ahi Poke with Sweet Onion, Avocado, Seaweed & Sesame with Wild Rice, 84

RICE
Kamala Grilled Salmon with Cucumber & Red Onion Salsa with Wild Rice & Sweet Chili Dipping Sauce, 109

RICE, WILD
Chicama Beef Stir-Fry with Onion, Bell Peppers, Garlic & Hand-made Oven Fries, 114

Ipanema Fresh Vegetable & Coconut Curry with Wild Rice, 74

Supertubos Paella with Chicken, Chorizo, Clams & Mussels, 99

Waimea Ahi Poke with Sweet Onion, Avocado, Seaweed & Sesame with Wild Rice, 84

Wild Coast Sausage with Scrambled Eggs, Cherry Tomatoes, Spinach and Wild Rice, 19

ROSEMARY
Imsouane Bay Spicy Shrimp with Orange & Seasonal Quinoa Salad, 66

La Chapelle Chicken Cassoulet with Olive, Sausage, Parma, Rosemary, Garlic, Cannellini Beans & Fennel, 117

La Torche Roasted Chicken with Lemon, Rosemary, Sautéed Brussels Sprouts & Smashed Celery Root, 88

Nijima Mixed Mushroom Ragout with Poached Egg, 29

Papara Marinated Squid with Chili Oil & Fresh Rosemary Served on Arugula Salad, 81

S

SAFFRON
Imsouane Bay Spicy Shrimp with Orange & Seasonal Quinoa Salad, 66

Supertubos Paella with Chicken, Chorizo, Clams & Mussels, 99

SALMON
Aleutian Wild Salmon and Quinoa Burger with Pesto and Two Eggs, 33

Kamala Grilled Salmon with Cucumber & Red Onion Salsa with Wild Rice & Sweet Chili Dipping Sauce, 109

Les Cavaliers Salmon, Spinach & Sun-Dried Tomato Crêpes, 38-39

SAUSAGE
La Chapelle Chicken Cassoulet with Olive, Sausage, Parma, Rosemary, Garlic, Cannellini Beans & Fennel, 117

Wild Coast Sausage with Scrambled Eggs, Cherry Tomatoes, Spinach and Wild Rice, 19

SAVORY
Grand Haven Bison Chili with Homemade Corn Tortilla Chips, 118

SEA BASS
Keramas Snapper with Stir-fried Ginger, Carrot, Asparagus & Broccolini, 91

Yumuri BBQ Sea Bass with Roasted Sweet Potatoes & Okra with Salsa Verde, 94

SEAWEED
Waimea Ahi Poke with Sweet Onion, Avocado, Seaweed & Sesame with Wild Rice, 84

SESAME SEEDS
Keramas Snapper with Stir-fried Ginger, Carrot, Asparagus & Broccolini, 91

Shimei Bay Omelet with Stir-fried Vegetables with Noodles, 26

Waimea Ahi Poke with Sweet Onion, Avocado, Seaweed & Sesame with Wild Rice, 84

SHALLOTS
Green Bowl Chicken Curry with Green Beans, Bell Peppers & Basil, 113

Keramas Snapper with Stir-fried Ginger, Carrot, Asparagus & Broccolini, 91

Playa Grande Grilled Pork Burger with Chimichurri Sauce & Sweet Potato Fries, 56

SHRIMP

Imsouane Bay Spicy Shrimp with Orange & Seasonal Quinoa Salad, 66

SNAPPER

Keramas Snapper with Stir-fried Ginger, Carrot, Asparagus & Broccolini, 91

SOY SAUCE

Chicama Beef Stir-Fry with Onion, Bell Peppers, Garlic & Hand-made Oven Fries, 114

Keramas Snapper with Stir-fried Ginger, Carrot, Asparagus & Broccolini, 91

Shimei Bay Omelet with Stir-fried Vegetables in Sesame Oil with Noodles, 26

Uchiumi Point Steak Salad with Edamame, Greens & Orange Sesame Dressing, 62

Trigg Point Sautéed Turkey Meatballs with Tomato & Onion Sauce on Spaghetti Squash, 103

SPINACH

Ditch Plains Green Pancakes with Onions, Chili & Spinach, 23

Laird's Beet & Berry Smoothie, 42

Laird's Lean Green Smoothie, 45

Les Cavaliers Salmon, Spinach & Sun-Dried Tomato Crêpes, 38-39

Superbank Chopped Chicken, Bacon, Egg, Spinach & Kale Salad, Asian Pear, Avocado, Cashew & Raisins with Curry Dressing, 78

Wild Coast Sausage with Scrambled Eggs, Cherry Tomatoes, Spinach and Wild Rice, 19

SQUID

Papara Marinated Squid with Chili Oil & Fresh Rosemary Served on Arugula Salad, 81

STEAKS

Chicama Beef Stir-Fry with Onion, Bell Peppers, Garlic & Hand-made Oven Fries, 114

Little Dume Grilled T-Bone Steak with Roasted Red Potatoes, Radishes with Fennel & Lemon Butter Sauce, 106

STEAKS, TRI-TIP

Uchiumi Point Steak Salad with Edamame, Greens & Orange Sesame Dressing, 62

STOCK, CHICKEN

La Torche Roasted Chicken with Lemon, Rosemary, Sautéed Brussels Sprouts & Smashed Celery Root, 88

STOCK, VEGETABLE

Nijima Mixed Mushroom Ragout with Poached Egg, 29

STRAWBERRIES

Half Moon Coffee and Cacao Granola with Natural Yogurt & Roasted Strawberries, 34

Higgins Mixed-Berry Cobbler, 129

Laird's Beet & Berry Smoothie, 42

SUGAR, COCONUT

Haiku Banana Bread with Grilled Pineapple, Yogurt & Mint, 126

Higgins Mixed-Berry Cobbler, 129

Kamala Grilled Salmon with Cucumber & Red Onion Salsa with Wild Rice & Sweet Chili Dipping Sauce, 109

SWEET POTATOES

Playa Grande Grilled Pork Burger with Chimichurri Sauce & Sweet Potato Fries, 56

Temae Spiny Lobster with Lemon Butter & Sautéed Sweet Potatoes, 100

Yumuri BBQ Sea Bass with Roasted Sweet Potatoes & Okra with Salsa Verde, 94

T

THYME

Grand Haven Bison Chili with Homemade Corn Tortilla Chips, 118

Kalo Nero Grilled Fig & Prosciutto Salad, 71

La Torche Roasted Chicken with Lemon, Rosemary, Sautéed Brussels Sprouts & Smashed Celery Root, 88

Nijima Mixed Mushroom Ragout with Poached Egg, 29

Playa Grande Grilled Pork Burger with Chimichurri Sauce & Sweet Potato Fries, 56

TILAPIA

Bondi Gluten-Free Breaded Tilapia with Zesty Arugula, Radish & Cucumber Salad, 121

First Point Grilled Tilapia Tacos with Kiwi, Pomegranate & Lime Salsa with Gluten-Free Tortillas, 65

Keramas Snapper with Stir-fried Ginger, Carrot, Asparagus & Broccolini, 91

TOMATO PASTE

Grand Haven Bison Chili with Homemade Corn Tortilla Chips, 118

TOMATOES

Anchor Point Shakshuka, Tomatoes, Peppers, Artichokes and Smoked Paprika with Eggs, 30

Grand Haven Bison Chili with Homemade Corn Tortilla Chips, 118

Honky's Squash Koftas in Masala Curry Sauce, 97

Ipanema Fresh Vegetable & Coconut Curry with Wild Rice, 74

Mundaka Tomato, Carrot & Turmeric Bisque Soup, 48

Trigg Point Sautéed Turkey Meatballs with Tomato & Onion Sauce on Spaghetti Squash, 103

TOMATOES, CHERRY

Chesterman Gluten-Free Toast, Bacon, Roasted Cherry Tomatoes & Guacamole, 41

Hanalei Bowl Chilled Avocado Soup with Summer Salsa, 55

Raglan Quinoa Salad with Grilled Corn, Mango, Tomatoes, Avocado & Goat Cheese, 77

METRIC CONVERSION CHART

VOLUME

1 tsp = ⅓ tablespoon = ⅙ fl oz = 4 ml

1 Tbsp = 3 teaspoons = ½ fl oz = 15 ml

⅛ cup = 2 tablespoons = 1 fl oz = 30 ml

¼ cup = 4 tablespoons = 2 fl oz = 50 ml

⅓ cup = ¼ cup plus 4 tsp = 2 ¾ fl oz = 75 ml

½ cup = 8 tablespoons = 4 fl oz = 125 ml

¾ cup = 10 tablespoons = 6 fl oz = 175 ml

1 cup = ½ pint = 8 fl oz = 250 ml

1 pint = 16 fl oz = 2 cups = 500 ml

1 quart = 32 fl oz = 2 pints

1 liter = 34 fl oz = 1 quart plus ¼ cup

1 gallon = 128 fl oz = 4 quarts

MASS

½ oz = 14 grams

2 oz = 57 grams

3 oz = 85 grams

4 oz = 113 grams

5 oz = 142 grams

6 oz = 170 grams

8 oz = 227 grams

10 oz = 283 grams

12 oz = 340 grams

16 oz = 454 grams

TEMPERATURE

450°F = 230°C

425°F = 220°C

400°F = 200°C

350°F = 180°C

325°F = 165°C

300°F = 150°C

250°F = 125°C

225°F = 110°C

ACKNOWLEDGMENTS

I feel exceptionally honored to be surrounded by so much talent and inspiration every day of my life. On the water, at home, and in business, I am constantly learning from those around me.

Central to my whole world are my girls; Gabrielle, Izabela, Reece and Brody. They are all powerful and independent spirits that are the loves of my life and support me throughout the challenges that life and my profession presents. Our family unit is tight and inclusive whatever the occasion, much of which happens takes place round the kitchen counter and the dinner table, so here we are with a window into what's being served.

I have published many recipes over the years, from Gabby's own, to chefs who are close friends, and the nutritional experts that I have met along the way. This book is a cohesive personal statement that reflects how fortunate I have been to travel around the planet, experience different cultures and their individual hospitality. I am extremely grateful to Esther at Assouline for immediately embracing the concept for *Fuel Up* and giving us free rein to create something fresh and bold, within such a luxurious format. I would also like to extend this gratitude to Prosper Assouline for its inclusion into the stunning Assouline library of work.

I am a creative at heart, particularly within my pursuits as an athlete and an innovator. When it comes to design and image making I defer to my friends and business partners; William and Jennifer Cawley. They put in the long hours, the eye for perfection, and the level of passion that a project like this requires. Together with their great friend and Malibu local, chef Sharla, the three of them produced every single detail of these immaculate recipes and the images that have resulted.

Lastly, a big shout out to everybody involved in my family of businesses. Each and every company I am involved with honestly reflect my life, the products, and manifestos that I live by—all of which are included in this book, from an introduction to Superfoods, to the equipment I surf, and the clothes that I wear. I have a very holistic and connected approach to life, so I hope you enjoy exploring this book and some of the surf spots around the globe.

Thank you again to all the fantastic human beings in my life. Bon appétit!

ABOUT THE AUTHORS

LAIRD HAMILTON is world-renowned as a waterman of the highest order, recognized as a primary influence behind many surfing innovations such as tow-in surfing, stand-up paddle boarding and hydrofoil boarding. Hamilton has transcended the sport of surfing to become an international fitness icon. Many of today's top professional athletes and celebrities look to Laird for training guidance, including instruction in his unique underwater resistance workouts. Laird has a passion for helping others live happy, healthy lives, as exhibited through his work with charities such as the Surfrider Foundation, Race Across America, Pipeline for a Cure for Cystic Fibrosis, and many others. Laird lives with wife Gabrielle Reece and their daughters on the Hawaiian island of Kauai six months out of the year during surfs' swell season and during the off season, in Malibu, California.

WILLIAM CAWLEY started his career in an advertising agency in Soho, London. This soon led to the establishment of his own design agency, which, over the subsequent 15 years, grew to more than 140 people. With a desire to "roll up his sleeves" once again, William relocated to Los Angeles and now leads a seasoned and illustrious group of brand engineers, Two Feet South, from his studio in Pacific Palisades. As a serial entrepreneur, he also operates an impressive portfolio of his own brands, products, and technology.

JENNIFER CAWLEY studied at the Art Institute of Chicago, after which she immediately established a notable reputation as an international freelance photographer. Throughout her career she has balanced highly technical commercial commissions with her passion for portraiture and fine art. Most recently, her skillset has broadened into film making, from concept to direction, shooting, and editing. As a co-owner of Two Feet South, Jennifer has enjoyed unlimited access to photographing Laird, something that requires immense versatility and skill with an arsenal of specialized equipment.

SHARLA BARRETT graduated from Pepperdine University with a BA in Humanities. She worked for many years in the arts—Houston Grand Opera and the Museum of Contemporary Art Los Angeles—before raising two daughters. She returned to school to become a licensed esthetician and cares deeply about the intrinsic effects of nutrition on the skin. A certified yoga teacher, she also believes in the deep relationship between physical activity and mental health. Cooking food that feeds the body and soul is a passion and lifestyle.

Previous pages: The swampy soils of our taro fields benefit from being in the wettest place on earth.
Following pages: My backyard for the other six months of the year: Paradise Cove, Malibu, California.

The information in this book is for informational purposes only. This book is not intended to be a substitute for professional medical advice, diagnosis or treatment.

CREDITS